CW01656336

Heather
Thank you for all your support.
Love
Josephine xx.

The *Revolutionary* Breakthrough

HOW TO TURN YOUR SETBACK INTO A PURPOSEFUL COMEBACK

Josephine S.N Kalagira

Breakfree Forever Publishing

Disclaimer

Author: Josephine S.N Kalagira

ISBN:978-1-9163736-1-7
Category: Motivational/Inspirational/Health

LIMITS OF LIABILITY/DISCLAIMER OF WARRANTY: The author and publisher of this book have used their best efforts in preparing this material. The author and publisher make no representation or warranties with respect to the accuracy, applicability or completeness of the contents. They disclaim any warranties (expressed or implied), or merchantability for any particular purpose. The author and publisher shall in no event be held liable for any loss or other damages, including but not limited to special, incidental, consequential, or other damages. The information presented in this publication is compiled from sources believed to be accurate. However, the publisher assumes no responsibility for errors or omissions. The information in this publication is not intended to replace or substitute professional advice. The author and publisher specifically disclaim any liability, loss, or risk that is incurred as a consequence, directly or indirectly, of the use and application of any of the contents of this work. Printed in the United Kingdom.

"To God Be The Glory For The Great Things He Has Done"

DEDICATION

I would like to dedicate my book to my dearest son Jayden.

At such a young age, you were able to be brave and strong throughout the worst times of my life. You have saved my life numerous times, whenever I have fainted, had panic attacks, and passed out completely, you have been my saviour. I know it was scary at times even when you never wanted to go to school because you thought you might find me dead, but you have been an amazing ROCK. I will forever be grateful for your life. You are and always will remain MY BIGGEST WHY.

Thank you for being so special, and wonderful always, I know there is no way I would have been the person I am today if it were not for you, I WILL ALWAYS LOVE YOU. Psalms 127:3.

ACKNOWLEDGEMENT

First and foremost, I would love to thank the almighty GOD for the gift of life, for all the trials and temptations, that I have confronted, accepted and embraced to shine through, and for enabling me to complete this amazing guided book that I believe will impact many lives through my personal walk. I had always wanted to inspire and empower others, but I never really knew how best to deliver this. I know HIS timing is the best to magnify and testify HIS GLORY. He has been my Lord, and Shepherd as indicated in Psalms 23.

I am speechless and really emotional about my Mum and Dad, as a parent myself, I can only imagine what you have gone through from a distance, the traumatic sleepless nights, knowing what I, your daughter was going through. Thank you for being there for me and for all your prayers. You both have been my rock and there is no way I could have pulled through without your tender loving care. Mum I want you to know that you are indeed one in a million and priceless. No one will ever take your place or be compared to you in my life. I am grateful that you continued to believe in me and stayed strong despite all the many challenges. I also want to thank my brothers and sisters who have been there for me without fail, I want you all to know that there is no way I would have made it this far without you. As the saying goes, 'we are scattered together through Ubuntu,' meaning, 'I am because we are.'

I would love to say a massive thank you to Linda and Mary from Holly Lodge Baptist Church, Shamira Robertson, Heather Bush, Altovise Pelzer, Hope Church Ipswich, Amanda Hutchinson, Dani Wallace, Michelle Watson, Keenda Sisouphanh, and Yasmin Sheikh for all your invaluable support. Thank you for listening, supporting, and encouraging. It was not an easy path, but we got there in the end.

My friends Susan and John, thank you for standing in the gap for me and my beloved son amidst all the storms in all abrupt situations. I would love to thank St. Mark's Roman Catholic School, Ipswich for your invaluable support towards my son on my behalf for ensuring that I was okay and never got tired of answering my calls and requests and made sure that my son was getting all the support he required which improved his progress at school.

David Sansom and family, and Cheryl Dodd your help and support have been highly appreciated.

Michelle Jones from Family First Christian Organisation, and Becky Ingram from Inside Out Charity Organisation. Thank you for helping and seeing me through my complex challenges to a positive change. You put a pure smile on my face by empowering and believing in me each week for a year.

Reverend Father Canon Mathew George, St Mary Magdalen Roman Catholic Church. From the bottom of my heart I thank you for organising the weekly visits for me to receive all the blessed sacraments that gave me hope and the feeling of God's presence in the comfort of my own home. I would also love to thank Minister Anna for her dedication and reassuring prayers.

Anna Parker-Naples. You gave me so much hope and believed in me when you granted me a full year's access to your Get Visible membership. Your knowledge, expertise and how you deliver your content has helped me tremendously. You are simply amazing and I have learned a lot from you being in your circle. I can't wait to get my podcast out there to the world.

Shamoni Kaur Gilani. Queen of Clarity Maven. Your help with my messaging clarity was invaluable and meant the world to me and boosted my confidence to go out there and share my message unapologetically.

Howard and Pearl, Mike Kasibo and the team of the Global Outreach Foundation MK, Laura Jeffrey and

Stephanie Thompson. Thank you so very much for all the selfless support and being there for me. Thank you to Sue Garbett from Suffolk Young Carers, and Lisa Johnson.

To everyone else I have not mentioned, please know that I thank you too for all your help and support.

May God bless you all abundantly.

CONTENT

FOREWORD

I first met Josephine when she was at a low point in her life, but even then what I noticed most about Josephine was her steadfast faith in God despite her challenges. I count it as a privilege to have been able to walk alongside Josephine during her recovery from the freak accident that changed her life. I witnessed first-hand the extreme debilitating pain and fatigue that she experienced daily that rendered her unable to cope with me visiting for an hour. In less than a year Josephine has made a truly miraculous transformation, turning her setback into a purposeful comeback. In this book Josephine will share with you how she has overcome chronic pain, depression and anxiety enabling you to do the same in your own life. You can be certain that what Josephine shares has the ability to change your situation, bringing healing and a new purpose, because she has experienced this for herself. Josephine is an inspirational and courageous woman of God who has shown perseverance in adversity. She has overcome great hurdles in her own life and continues to demonstrate her ability to deal with life's challenges, both big and small. I am certain this book will inspire you to make the necessary changes in your own life so that you can also be transformed. Above all I am sure that Josephine's story will help you to understand that God can turn even the darkest situation into a power for good.

Michelle Jones
Senior Family Coordinator Family First

INTRODUCTION

This book has been inspired and written after the most traumatic personal injury experience I encountered in April 2017 and indicating how my life changed in the blink of an eye. Who knew shopping would be so dangerous?

I felt that there was no other way I would be able to sit down with someone and take them through most of my experiences apart from putting it into writing, and through this way, more people and generations to come would benefit from these experiences in my writing. This would explain what I underwent and how I managed to overcome and manage the situation despite all the challenges. I am blessed to be able to overcome or even find a solution or two to take away with you or for you to relate to your personal circumstance and be enlightened to learn or create some kind of awareness for you.

This book is there to inspire you, give you hope, faith, motivate, educate you and encourage you if you are undergoing pain, struggling with physical disability that is either visible or invisible, had a personal injury, chronic illness, frustration, depression, anxiety, PTSD, confused or unsure of where to turn to for help. To reassure you, that there is always a way out at the end of the darkest tunnel if you decide to stay true to yourself and listen to that little tiny voice, and strive to shine through it all. Therefore, I feel that, this book can relate to anyone. I say so because at any one point, it is possible to feel stranded and stuck or under some kind of a challenging constraint.

I believe that after reading this book you will feel some relief, be inspired, have learned some simple coping strategies and tips, evaluate yourself and look at how you have been managing or thinking things over and perhaps consider an alternative path and approach.

I also believe that you might think of someone you feel may benefit from reading this book who you could recommend the book to. Here, we can all learn. You see, I have come to realise that if you do have some burning message that you would like to deliver after so much pain, difficulty and struggle, but cannot find the exact way, writing is one of those therapies that can be non-judgemental. It enables you to express yourself in the moment and being congruent with yourself is so rewarding beyond measure. Writing from the heart, 'the truth, and only the truth,' will provide you with the comfort of what you get to choose and know that there's always someone out there willing to help and support you.

In this book, you will identify that, through writing and sharing with others, you would be creating room for your inner healing as well as being a resourceful tool for others waiting to hear your message so they can be inspired and empowered to overcome their personal setbacks.

CHAPTER ONE

About Me

I come from a Roman Catholic Christian home where I was shown and had instilled the core values of Christianity. I am proud of my religion and faith. At quite an early age, my love for being a dedicated Christian began from having ordained priests, reverends, nuns and a bishop visiting our home for prayers. Looking back now, I understand the message they were carrying and sharing with us and what I personally perceived. Even though I wasn't so dedicated, I knew I had to say prayers each day and recite a rosary mainly in May and October. At an early age, I was experiencing encounters through dreams with various messages of what I needed to do, or what was going to happen. I was being shown how to do anything I wanted to do but never really did and each time I implemented it, I would get exactly what I wanted. I was shown so many things that no-one had told me about and because I knew what was happening and what was going on, from that point I remember telling my parents that I wanted to be a nun.

I remember people asking me why I wanted to take that path but I felt directed each time and only I knew if I could be a reverend sister (Nun). I would commit most of my time to serving the Lord and receiving more messages. My parents were very supportive of this. I even attended schools that were mission orientated. I was bought books about what I was going into such as the 'Daughters of Mary Bannabikira Sisters Bwanda' and 'The Good Samaritan Sisters Nalukolongo,' both in Uganda.

I remember I was so into this calling that I made applications where I was told that after leaving high school, I would be considered. It was like a dream come true receiving letters from them confirming what they had told me. So I kept this so close and it meant so much to me but of course, as a teenager, things happened and my perspective of listening to how I was being led by the Holy Spirit changed to following what others were saying and believed in, so I went along too.

When it came to saying prayers, I would come up with anything that gave excuses, and every time I would be revealed anything I would say it was just a dream.

I am so grateful that the revelations and encounters did not stop until when I got reunited back into starting prayers with dedication and determination years later, and to understand why I was created and why I was getting them, which made me super grateful. And now, I am extremely privileged to be supporting and healing to helping others to heal, by getting them back on their feet, by sharing what I know and understanding how it will resonate with them. I feel that I have so much to share and talk about on this topic but I believe I will be able to do so in my next book.

Anyway, let me tell you a bit about how I moved from Uganda to the UK.

This happened superfast and it wasn't anything that I had planned in advance.

It was approximately one month after I had finished high school, around late November of 2004. Between this period and the 21st December 2004, all the paperwork and the UK visa were confirmed. As you can imagine, my birthday was on the 22nd December, so this was the best present ever.

I left Uganda on the 31st December 2004 and I arrived in the UK on 1st January 2005. Like anyone else would be, I was super excited for the new adventure, but oh my goodness me...did it not hit me? It was so cold and I had never experienced anything like it before. At some point I thought my teeth were going to fall out. I just couldn't understand how everyone spoke, and in my head, I was like, 'this is not how I was taught to speak at school,' it was far from it. I then remembered the times I was encouraged to speak English and I took it for granted, and so here I was facing the reality of the real need to speak it. In fact, I was even scared to say a word and my accent was so strong, so I found it challenging to express myself. I imagined how I was going to live here and cope but thankfully, with perseverance and determination, I knew I had to get through it.

Something else that challenged me was the food itself, goodness me! It did not have any taste and the water made me feel sick each time. I was used to spring water or pot water that had some flavour and aroma, and I couldn't find it here. I remember speaking to my family about it and my Mum was like, in my language, 'munange obuzaliiro sibukuliro era bwogenda ebuly'ambwa naawe olina okuyiga okulya embwa,' meaning 'you can't always be in the same place you were born, and when you go to a different culture you have to adjust as well'. She added, 'you have to eat to live as opposed to feel the taste…I then knew it was time to dance to the same tune as everyone else.

I wasn't so long in the UK and moved to Germany where I lived for just over three years. During this time I would travel back and forth to the UK on road adventures and by air. It was so much fun, the stopovers in different countries, the food, and being on various ferries.

Back to Germany. As soon as I got there, again, it was a brand new world. I had been adjusting to the English language and was now living in a non-English speaking country. I'll leave you to visualise this for a second; do you see what I am on about? Exactly! That was me. Oh my goodness me. I remember spending about three months indoors eating eggs, not because I did not have the money to go and buy what I wanted to eat but because I was worried about how to communicate for what I wanted. This is what shyness and being insecure about being yourself does. I would never wish anyone to go through this ever. But after some time, I made some friends who went to the same church as I did and I was able to open up to them. They really helped me and I started going out more, which boosted my confidence.

I was shocked when I went and applied for a job within the British Army barracks and got it. What made everyone surprised was that I went dressed as though I was the CEO for a customer service assistant role. My dressing up was obviously appreciated.

It made me happy and I never stopped dressing up. In fact, I was nominated and put on the garrison's notice board demonstrating how everyone should be dressed up for work. On top of what I was doing in my job role, I remember walking into my manager's office and she was touch-typing super quickly. I was intrigued by this and wanted to learn more about how she acquired this skill as I was keen when it came to personal development. As soon as she explained how to get on the course and where, I created time and enrolled on a course in computing. I think it was called ECDL - European Computer Driving License. I was able to complete and successfully pass all modules in six months; it's like I was on fire.

This gave me a lot of courage to keep going and believe in myself a bit. Each time I wanted to go on another higher level on something I was passionate about, I would ask some people around me who were far more knowledgeable than I was and who had finished their degrees to seek their approval. They would say it was too difficult to do university studies and that I wouldn't manage it.

If you have negative people in your life talking you out of your heart's desire, you need to take your power back in order to step into your purpose otherwise, you will always be in the same place. This is because, in most cases, they will be progressing and you will be left stagnant and frustrated which causes a lot of regrets in the future. I knew deep down what I was capable of and what I really wanted, so I went on to do lots of courses here and there that helped me tremendously because I knew this is what I wanted.

Around July to August 2008, I moved back to the UK, Oxfordshire, where I lived for just over a year and then moved to Ipswich in Suffolk because the father of my son had left the army to pursue his studies at the now University of Suffolk. I had to leave my job roles to support him as there was no reason for me to stay there any longer. The move happened unexpectedly for me as in less than two months, I had to pack and move.

Upon moving there, I had only two weeks money for the flat deposit and after that, there was not any money saved in advance so I had to go out and find a job that would be able to cover the rent whilst waiting for my months money to come, the quickest I found was one packing onions. The job I got required me to pack onions. When I applied for this role, I didn't know what it involved and found out on the day I turned up for work. This caused me to hate eating onions. I stayed there because I was desperate for the money. During this time, I spoke to my previous employer enquiring about if there were any local centres they had that I could transfer to. Upon coming back to me, I was told that there were two places where they needed someone but it was over an hour away. I asked whether I could go and view both places and see which one I would prefer to work at and I picked one.

After just over three weeks, I left the onion place. The money from my previous role came through including my holiday pay and I was all good for rent and transport to and from work in my new job where I was so welcomed. It was, however, such a challenge to go and come back each day, working long hours and driving at the same time and it was costly on petrol too. This called me to look for a job closer to where I lived after four months.

After I had settled in, I took on extra roles that required me to do a few hours and I also got two more jobs as the bills were extremely high and I had other personal responsibilities. This was so exhausting and I thought about looking into personal development to get more freedom and money while working less to balance my life around. As I was planning all of this I fell pregnant with my God answered prayer of a special son and gave birth to him in January 2012. He came at the right time when I needed him the most after trying for over five years. This was pure joy, and holding him in my arms and looking into his eyes kept me going. This is because I was experiencing some unusual and really challenging signals in my life that I was choosing to ignore, under look and even sweep what I was going through at the time under the carpet which wasn't going well and I knew this wasn't sitting right with me but I remember having so many questions and didn't know how to face the answers. My mindset was really poor due to many circumstances and consequences as you would imagine.

There was a day when I had just returned from a visit to Uganda with my 6 month old son that I looked at him and the thought came to me. I need to be more, I deserve more and to do more so that when he grows up he would have something to be proud of me.

In October 2012, it was such a chilly day but I decided to walk to the local university to make some enquiries about looking into my future and to find out how I could progress academically as I was confident that this would be the answer.

Upon walking into the university's information zone, I was asked what I wanted to be helped with by a friendly adviser, but I wasn't confident at all and I felt so shy to express myself in a way that I really wanted to. Even though I was panicking and felt like 'what am I really doing here?' I picked myself up and I said I wanted to do a course in nursing or social work simply because it's what everyone else was talking about and I had been working as a support worker before I had my son. The adviser asked for my GCSE and A level results, which I had handy. She went and looked through via a system that translated my results as they were from Uganda. She happily told me that I did qualify to be on any of the courses I liked. This made me smile, however, I was told that because my results were over five years past when I completed them, I needed to undergo an access to higher education course before starting the university. Well at my age, it was not for me. I didn't quite want to do that because it would have been one to two years before starting university and I was told that I needed to start this a year after as that years' intake was late in.

As the adviser kept browsing through my documents, she landed on a certificate where I had done an online course in Business Management. She asked me about some of the modules I did and what I had learned from them. I was able to explain and she asked me whether it would be something I would consider pursuing further. Oh my days! This was like a dream come true. This is because it reminded me why I undertook this course after I had been for my work appraisal and when I openly told them about what I wanted to do in the future, shockingly, they laughed at me and said, 'who would I manage?' I must admit, this made me cry and made me think I wasn't enough simply because it had come from a senior person who didn't believe in me. But I believed in myself deep down.

It was from total frustration that one day I hoped to be self-employed or manage a team and work my way up. The adviser got intrigued and asked whether I would be happy to talk to the head of department in that area and check whether they would accept me on the course. I said yes but I had my son with me who had started crying and wanted to breastfeed. In the meantime, a team of senior lecturers came and asked me to go into another room and they asked me a lots of questions which I was able to answer to the best of my knowledge while I was rocking the pram for my son to be quiet. One of the questions that I found challenging was when I was asked how I would manage with full time studying and having a young child who was still breastfeeding and didn't have childcare. From my answers I was told that they were pleased to offer me a conditional place to do my degree in Business Management with HR Management – I was over the moon!

From this point now, even though I was super excited, I didn't have any money to get the ball rolling as I had just come from Uganda. The process for applying for a student loan I was told would take longer than normal for everything to come through. I immediately had to contemplate to check that what I was going into was right simply because of my son. A few people I confided in told me that I would never finish the university course, I wouldn't understand the language and that it would be too advanced for me and that the course was so difficult that what I wanted to do wasn't something that could be done by someone from my ethnicity and that I would never have a job after that. I had a passion for this course but I was scared. I asked my Mum and told her what had happened to me. She knew the number of times that I deferred this course every time I was offered it and after going through UCAS and all the hassle that comes across completing this and that, she said on this occasion I had to make a commitment and go ahead with the course.

As we confide in the people we care about concerning something we are passionate to do, that we are going to do it and then eventually we don't, it can be so annoying when some not so patient people give up on us or don't take us seriously. Mum advised me on my worry and my young son that at least I had breastfed her grandson exclusively for six months and that he would be breastfed in the evenings when I came back. This was reassuring and I was getting a step closer.

Another tug of war was when I started to look for child-care providers. I remember it was a Wednesday in 2012 and other students had already started on a Monday so every-thing else that I had to do was in a rush in order to start university. Luckily I found a childcare provider who had a space for full time hours that I required but the charges were over £900 each month. I had to confide in the manager and told her of my financial situation and that I wasn't able to pay that amount upfront. She was so understanding and we made an agreement for me to pay for that month and the following month in full after the date I had promised. Remember, my application for student finance here wasn't even in however, I was determined and made a commitment that this was the route I had to take no matter what it would cost me.

It was a challenging situation having to meet all the other bills for my son and myself but once I knew my son was safe I went and confirmed my place at the university. I didn't even take into account the other people who had tried to talk me out of it because I prioritised myself and my WHY was strong enough.

My insecurities were around English not being my first language and whether I would get a job. I was a mature student but I connected with some close classmates who helped me get through this. At times when I was skint they helped financially too. I started to hear the voice of my previous manager who had asked me, 'who would I manage?'

I was concerned about whether I could get a job in the meantime as I was breastfeeding. It could get really uncomfortable at times and the breast pads I had would be used up. Some people would even spot the visible marks on my tops and this was really embarrassing but I was resilient.

My attendance was really good but I was struggling. Whenever we were given an assignment it would take me days to do or put into a concept and I wondered why. I remember hearing a talk about the things I was going through and the struggles I was experiencing. I needed to see someone to talk about it and so I took action. When I did and after an assessment, I was told that I was dyslexic and the assessor even wondered how I had managed up to this point. I was glad that I had sought advice and this helped me to get the support that I really needed and it boosted my confidence and got me back on track.

I never looked back despite all the challenges. I showed up to various workshops that helped me with re-writing my CV and my application for internships that supported my transferable skills. When it came to applying for jobs, I was always seen as someone who was so much more aware, and this made me stand out from the crowd. I made myself known and open to recruiters so that whenever they were recruiting for a job, they would see me as the best person to be contacted. I became a student ambassador and was featured on websites and in brochures; I am even on the front cover of the Vision 2020 magazine for the university!

I graduated with a 2:1 in BA Hons. in Business Management with Human Resources Management, which I was extremely proud of. I was able to invite my parents over from Uganda and they came to attend and celebrate the incredible day with me. This is all I had wished for on that special day.

After my last semester, I was employed by the same university as a result of my visibility and being proactive on a temporary contract. This did not take time but courage. I had to prove that I was the best person for the role. Whilst in this role, I had the privilege of meeting Ed Sheeran who shook my hand; he even called me mate! I loved this and had I not taken this role on, I doubt whether I would have met him.

When this ended, I was employed by another organisation where I first worked as an intern and I believe I stood out the most on this basis. But because I had a young son who had started reception class when I started this job, this could not permit me to work the full-time hours I wanted. I asked for part-time hours which I was granted and I thought I had landed on my feet. Little did I know that the hours I was given were for someone who had gone for her maternity leave. Within a year she requested to return so this meant that my time with this company had to come to an end. Yeah, I was devastated but it was no choice of my own.

I moved on my next job was my dream come true; it felt like home right from my interview It was about an hour from where I lived but I was more than happy to travel. My work colleagues and manager were heavenly. They knew about my reasons for going to university and my dyslexia and they supported me entirely.

I was offered the job before I got home on a fixed-term contract. I accepted the offer even before sorting out arrangements for my son. My job finished at 5pm each evening which was the same time that his after school club finished. As it would take me at least an hour to drive back from Ipswich, I realised I had a problem to overcome. It was a bit of a challenge but I took a leap of faith. I eventually found the right place for him where they organised to pick him up from school at 15:15pm and look after him until 6pm when I picked him up. There was a hook in this arrangement though. For every minute that I was late it would cost me £1 extra. Despite this, I signed a contract and

I ended up paying quite a few extra pounds due to traffic and other unforeseen circumstances.

I was so happy at my the job. My reviews were promising and within two months I had a few meetings with my manager who told me how proud she was of me and that I had received positive feedback from the rest of the team. Even though there were some areas of improvement, all was great. I was nicknamed 'sunshine.' I must admit, this made my days worthwhile. I also kept in touch with some of my previous colleagues keeping them up to date with how I was finding the place and how my role was going and my forecast on the future.

I had started looking around for houses and schools as I wanted to move closer without anyone's pressure; I can recall this like it was yesterday.

It was Friday 21st April 2017. I had another meeting with my manager. This was to discuss how she was going to confirm to me on the following Monday that my contract was to be extended or made permanent as she felt that I was an incredible asset to the team. I was permitted to go home earlier on that day but little did I know what would follow after that!

As you know, I worked 9 to 5 Monday to Friday with an approximate drive of one hour from where I lived. If you are a parent and have this same routine you will clearly understand what it feels like when you have planned to have a lie in on a Saturday. Leaving work early on that Friday I was super excited and was looking forward to the weekend. I had loud music playing in my car on my way to pick up my son from his after school club. After I'd picked him up I decided to quickly do some shopping so I did not have to wake up so early in the morning.

The accident occurred within the supermarket in the presence of my five year old son.

I was around the fridges aisle and I had bent to pick up a yoghurt when suddenly an employee of the store who happened to be pushing and pulling two cages full of goods hit me from behind with the cage he was pushing... Yes!...and OUCH! This caused me to scream in pain and I stumbled.

"You alright?" I heard the assistant say. For like a minute I did not know what was going on as the area on my body that had been hit started to feel numb. My son was in shock and scared and he said that he was sorry and that he hadn't been able to save me. The employee rushed to push the first cage through a set of double doors and quickly came to pick up the other one. After like a minute or two, I started to feel sharp pains in my entire leg and the area where the cage had hit me on my back and right foot. It may have looked or seemed as something minor at the time but little did I know then that this was to have a negative impact on my life for some considerable time.

The pain continued to feel more severe and so uncomfortable. I left everything else that I had intended to buy and took what I had already picked up to the till. On my way I saw the employee who had knocked me over. He was peeping through a window staring at me! When I tried to call him he hid under a table inside the no entry area. I was fuming! At this point I had to take off my shoe as I was wearing high heels and due to the increasing pain, I was finding it difficult to walk.

I managed to limp to the till where I asked to speak to the manager of the store before paying for the goods that I had picked up before the injury. About two minutes later the person who had knocked into me with the cage came out and opened up another till to start serving customers. Shockingly, this is when I realised he was actually the store manager as he was wearing a name badge that identified him as such.

When I went to have a word with him it was like I was invisible to him and he was not helpful at all. Given the fact that he had caused the accident I found his manner towards me extremely unprofessional. I told him that I needed information from him regarding how to make a complaint and report the accident. I couldn't believe his attitude! He simply pointed to some leaflets near the exit and told me to pick one up on my way out before turning away from me! I was shocked and very upset at his lack of interest. I couldn't believe this was happening.

I collected my items and stumbled to the exit, picking up a couple of the leaflets on my way out to the car. On the way, I dropped some of the shopping which my son quickly picked up for me. Once in the car I picked up one of the leaflets and noticed a customer service contact number for the supermarket's Head Office. As I started to call the number on the leaflet I wondered if I would be able to drive home with my injured foot. I was worried that I could be a danger to not only myself and my son, but to other road users as well.

I finally managed to get through to the customer service department and explained to the agent exactly what had happened to me, especially the part about the manager's negative attitude, his lack of duty of care and his failure to complete an accident incident form. The agent recorded all of the details, gave me a reference number and told me that all the details would be passed to the area manager and I would receive a response within ten days. Nobody ever got back to me.

I also made sure that the local police were informed of the incident and obtained a reference from them as well but I was advised that as this had happened in the store, I should follow up with the supermarket going forward as they needed to take the appropriate action according to their policies and procedures. I knew I was doing the right thing because for me, this was unfair treatment straightway.

Whilst going through these painful and traumatic challenges, I was confident that the supermarket was highly responsible for the accident because of the following:

i. They breached their duties in accordance with section 2(2) of the Occupiers Liability Act 1957 in that they failed to take all reasonable care to ensure that visitors to their premises would be reasonably safe in using their premises for the purposes of which they are invited or permitted to be there.
ii. This caused / permitted their employee to manoeuvre the caged trolleys in a reckless manner with no visibility of where he was heading to and as such to became or remained a danger to visitors to their premises.
iii. Failed to employ competent members of staff who presented an obvious, foreseeable, and serious risk to visitors' health and safety.
iv. Failed to institute or enforce any or adequate systems of inspection whereby the mismanagement of trolleys might have been noted before my accident.
v. The supermarket was vicariously liable for the actions of their employee for failing to ensure the manner in which the trolleys were being handled

was safe and therefore exposed me to a foreseeable risk of injury.

vi. My five year old son had to witness the pain I am in as well as noticing the incident, which he has not forgotten about. It is clear that if the employee can run over me who is big enough to be seen, how about if their employee had run over my son who is considerably smaller? He has continuously asked me about this but I have had to keep reassuring him of how glad I am that it was me that was hit as opposed to him.

Before liability was accepted by the supermarket, I was asked to provide names and addresses of any witnesses. Surely, this got on my nerves due to the fact that as I was not paying attention to who was shopping at that particular time I believe other customers were not too. The store was also not busy as this happened really quickly. If you ever get in a situation like this, please make note of any eye witnesses and take pictures too if you can.

Upon getting home, the pain had increased. My foot and ankle were getting so swollen and the painkillers I had taken weren't kicking in. I called the emergency 999 number and told them what had happened. They took me through some questions and advised me to go to A&E at the local hospital. On arriving, it took hours before I was seen. When they did I was told that it was a soft tissue injury and that the swelling and pain would settle down after seventy-two hours. They said that I didn't need an x-ray done and was advised take the painkillers that the A&E doctor had prescribed for me.

As per the doctor's instructions, I carried on taking the medication but I hardly slept that night and was restless with so much pain with pins and needles shooting through my leg and foot. Saturday was the same and Sunday was no better. My foot and leg were so swollen and sore and I couldn't bear the pain anymore.

Unable to drive, I called a taxi and returned to the hospital where I saw another consultant. His diagnosis was a soft tissue injury of the Achilles tendon. Again, no x-ray was done and I was told that the pain could take a good few weeks but he could not be specific as all injuries differ. He recommended that I be referred for physiotherapy and I was also provided with crutches.

Months on, I still have severe pain through my leg and foot, especially on the heel with sharp pins and needles and muscular spasms. I sometimes can't feel my toes and I'm unable to make any movement with my leg or stand on my injured foot. This leaves me restless during the day and night and severely limits my ability to do things which would not have been the case if it was not for this injury caused by that supermarket.

My son, at the age of five, started being a young carer. He kept blaming himself for my injuries because he had not saved me. The authorities threatened to take him away from me a few times because I wasn't coping well. I felt judged, not valued or respected. I was on high doses of medication and kept being mis-diagnosed with various conditions. The fact that I had someone who was under my care and whom I couldn't look after was another worry. With not having enough food to eat, the food banks were a God send. I remember one particular night we had to sleep in the dark and cold because we had no money for lighting or heating. I felt that the only way out was to end my life. I couldn't see the light at the end of the tunnel. I was called names and lies were told about me.

And I couldn't help myself. Life was hard. I remember that one day when I found myself at the hospital in the resuscitation department where my life nearly ended. A few people came to visit me and my son was brought to me. I looked into his eyes. He gave me a cuddle and he said he loved me so much and he missed me. I felt the same but I had so many voices fighting within me. I was blaming myself. I didn't feel worthy. I didn't know how to get back on my feet. I had a lot of anger about this person who had caused my injuries. I had issues with my solicitor as well. One friend called my name and said, "Josephine, if you die now, where would that leave your son?" She, in not so many words, implied that I was being selfish.

I somehow realized that enough was enough. I had to take my power back from those I thought would help and be there for me. I started visualising what I wanted and deserved and above all, I had to be the best mum to my special son. We had been through so much together and ending my life wasn't going to be the answer however much it was coming through so strong.

I gradually started to write things down; how I wanted them and WHY, and what it would mean to me when I had achieved that goal and the steps that I needed to take. Anything that was out of my control I found a way of dealing with and rather than being angry and sad about who didn't do what and why they didn't, I chose to accept them and implement empathy. I chose to rise and speak up about my suffering, pain and struggles in a way that best defined me without allowing someone else to speak for me and because this was a great way to manage and cope, it made me feel so much better and alive. I was able to develop my eight pillar signature approach to help and support others. I accepted help and took one day at a time. I looked into personal development and invested into myself to learn more from the best experts. I chose to show up, reach out and believe in never ever to give up on me again.

I now suffer with chronic pain with symptoms of complex pain regional syndrome (CPRS), sciatic nerve pain, and weight and postural imbalances.

At this stage I should say that it is paramount that you get to reflect on your situation and your previous one and ensure that you make a record of every single bit of information of what you are doing or missing out on that you used to do and enjoyed on a daily basis. It is very important you get into a routine of doing so because as time goes by we can tend to forget the exact details of an incident and those details may be needed for reference in the future. I found this very helpful and when writing this book, I relied on much of those details and information from my own notes.

Having been off sick due to this injury, I applied for an Access to Work grant. The total sum of the support grant would be £4363.55 with effect from the date I was injured. It took a lot of time to make this application and arrange a meeting for the assessor to come and visit me at my workplace to carry out the assessment before being offered the grant. The terms and conditions to this were for the assessor to critically review the report and the recommendation with my manager, have this agreed and then sign and send this back. As I was unable to drive or get to work to attend the assessment (it is quite a distance from Ipswich to Witham) I was not able to complete this which resulted in my claim being dismissed due to the limited time scale to review and send it back. It would have been too costly if I'd tried to go over using a taxi.

Having not been employed long enough with my employer, I was advised that I would not be paid any statutory sick pay which meant loss of earnings, money that I entirely relied on.

I was also at the brink of losing my job due to this injury and other complementary bonuses that came with having it. The fact that I was not going to be paid sick pay for the time I was off was going to leave me in a financial mess. I was also worried about my job as I was still on a temporary contract and had not yet been made a permanent member of staff. I just could not stop worrying and I visualised my dream job slipping away from me just like that.

Being a single parent with a five year old son in my condition at that particular moment was so hard. I was not able to drive anywhere and my son had missed out on quite a few activities that he attended during the week due to my immobility. Using taxis to get around when needed and also to take my son to school and pick him up was so expensive costing approximately £135 per week and certainly not something I had planned for on a daily basis. This again was causing me so much stress both psychologically and physically and making me feel depressed.

I started to borrow money from friends but did not know how and when I could pay them back. Something you should be careful about because it is really easy to get yourself into heavy debt due to late payment charges on credit cards and other monthly bills.

I also started to experience my hands and palms being so sore and bruised due to not being used to using crutches. I had a few falls as well and I remember breaking my son's new tablet by dropping it on the floor. It had cost £90. I was really frustrated by this and I hid it from him when he was searching for it. I just could not say that it was completely broken and wouldn't turn back on any more. I also broke some glasses and cups in the process of trying to get something to eat. Also, due to the structure of my property, there were a few steps and heavy double doors which are not so easily accessible for anyone with some disability or injury of any kind. These created a lot of distress and struggles in so many ways, restricting the things I used to do so freely.

Remember, my entire family lives in Uganda. Since my injury, they had been so worried about me resulting in me making calls to reassure them even though deep down I knew I was not well. Those calls helped to relieve my stress level but they came at a cost. Within a short period of time I had spent close to £600 on telephone calls!

Throughout this dark period in my life I had friends who came around to give a helping hand when I was in so much pain and could hardly get up to go and pick my son up from school, who assisted with my house chores like taking the bin out, shopping, and anything else I had trouble doing. I remember doing some shopping online but the quality of the products I purchased were not to my taste and I ended up wasting my money when they were not eaten. So real friends deserve golden stars and are to be cherished forever. I could not thank them enough.

Now on top of the cost of my phone calls to Uganda there were gas and electricity bills to consider. I noted that as I was indoors all the time, my bill costs went up and I had to top up my electricity and gas even during the week or use the emergency credit. Even when I had to make enquiries about something, I had to use my phone which sometimes took around 10 - 30 minutes which added to my financial burden.

I felt that due to some of these reasons, I was at the verge of breaking down as this was not something I had anticipated to happen, especially in a public area within a supermarket. So I wanted to make them aware that when coming up with their compensation settlement, those reasons should not be omitted and should be taken into consideration as part of my injury. Be watchful and aware if you are or know someone who may need to know this and is dealing with a similar challenge.

It all ended up by me taking action, speaking my truth, accepting help and when all of this was in play, I felt listened to, supported and heard. All this resonated with my body, heart and soul. Great things started happening and people were reaching out to me and were giving me great feedback after I had spoken with them. This gave me hope and courage that I could help other people as well in the same way despite what they may be dealing with.

Because of my tenacity and passion to not be defined by my circumstances, I got featured in the local newspaper and also in other articles of 'Our Voice Matters.' Because of what I had been through and encountered, I came across so many other people who were in the same situation but in fear and not sure of how to express themselves, hence the reason for my calling as a 'Setback to Come Back Coach' where I help ambitious people who are struggling with physical and/or emotional challenges to have a safe space where they can be heard so I that I can support them through their setback and empower them to come back stronger than ever before. I feel strongly empowered to help women who have lost their self-esteem due to any physical trauma and who need that emotional support to get back on their feet with confidence to enjoy their desired lives. And I know that if you are struggling and would love to feel better without blaming anyone else, only You Can Make It Happen…That's what I personally did and I know you too CAN.

In the following chapters, I am going to be sharing with you how I managed to accept whatever it is that I was going through to me shining now wholeheartedly with my body and soul, and this is what I implement when using my own 1to1 proven system approach to those I support in a personalised way depending on their personal level of support required. I know you might not even know where you are in your life right now, or have no idea of what you would want to do and achieve if you are in constant pain and struggling with emotional stress and anxiety but I can promise you that each chapter for me shifted me, and elevated me onto the next level which helped with my recovery. I believe you will find and gain a lot of value in each chapter.

CHAPTER TWO

Take Time Out

I am not so sure about you, but at several points I felt like I was a prisoner of my situation because of what happened to me. Never had it crossed my mind that I had to take time out to set myself up from scratch. I knew I had tried all I could, but everything else was revolving around the same thing. Basically I could not fly without wings. Well, I acknowledged that I had been through all that I have encountered, seen all medical experts and kind of now understood my condition. I was aware that over assuming and straining that things would be the same as before my accident; it wasn't as straightforward as I thought it would be or I wasn't being true to myself.

I remember talking about wanting to do a course on neutral linguistic programming to work on my mindset but could not afford it however, one professional found it, bought it and presented it to me. Alongside reading the book, listening to motivational speakers and inspiring content, this allowed me to truly know who I was through self-actualisation. And being aware that, if I concentrated on focussing on what could go wrong rather than right, then I would be attracted to just that. From this point, I slowly surrendered to agree and embrace taking time out, paused and pressed the start button again. I also realised that it's never too late to start over. If I was not happy yesterday of my current situation, I had to ensure that I try something different today, not to stay stuck but do better and get back on track.

I started brainstorming, developing ideas and researching as well as connecting with the right people. I did this by attending local events, conferences and by social media. The fact that I was still struggling with my life, I knew I could not get back into a normal job, sit for very long hours and my medication as well played a big key role in being a hindrance. I was able to convince myself that I was more than ready to start from scratch. By saying this, even though I did, there were lots of ups and downs in order to progress but I kept on top of it as I wanted a change in my life and I knew I was destined for greatness.

Some of the things that happened to me were encouraging, especially when I took out my 2020 Vision university catalogue. I was like, this did not happen by mistake. So, I was enabled to stay focussed, my vision and goals were bigger than everything I could and couldn't see. I had to make tough decisions to make it. I undertook various courses such as: counselling and listening skills, complementary therapies, sewing and design, confidence and well-being, diploma in life coaching and mindfulness. I was nominated for the Suffolk Adult Award 2019 Inspirational Student and now enrolled on a creative mentoring course to enable me concentrate and be able to relax and calm my mind down. This is because I was experiencing severe headaches as I was trying to think of too much by wanting to get to the end of the tunnel before taking one step at a time.

People may laugh or say all kinds of words against you but if you indeed are listening to the tiny voice within you before being judged, you would be able to happily make decisions very easily without minding anyone else other than where your calling and purpose are destined. Whilst undergoing this process, choose the people you associate yourself with wisely, who to trust, and not sharing that much. If in doubt, ensure that social media does not blow you away by being carried over; you will lose friends or be seen differently within your area. People may destroy your image, stain your personality but that can't take away your good deeds because no matter how they describe you, you will still be admired by those who really know you better. This is what helped me to take time out and was always reminded by it. So for me, this is the difference that my learning has made.

I came into contact with Realise Futures after I visited the Job Centre and saw a booklet that had various courses. I was in a terrible state with my mental health condition after a terrible supermarket injury where I was knocked with a fully loaded cage. I was struggling to cope with life and other life-changing episodes with poor mobility and the loss of my dream job with Essex Fire Services within their HR Department because as a result of the injury, I was unable to drive. Having a young son of five years of age who looked up to me, I was a total mess and had lost my sense of belonging, with no confidence at all. My self-esteem was affected and certainly what I had become was shocking to me as well.

Deep down I knew I had to do something to change my life and for my son not to be heavily affected by my situation. I was worried sick, could not concentrate, in severe pain, restless and on strong painkillers. If you know someone who has ever dealt with or suffered depression, chronic pain and PTSD, you will understand all the symptoms. I kept hearing harmful voices which were scary to the extent that I overdosed myself and ended up in hospital.

I had to find a way of overcoming, managing and diverting myself from this situation. I enrolled in two courses; one was sewing as this helped me to forget everything else happening around me and concentrate on a given task which intuitively worked well, and the other course was in Listening and Counselling Skills.

Upon taking these courses, my tutor undertook an assessment for me including a health and safety plan as I couldn't bear weight and had to use crutches. I was open to share with her what I was undergoing and as I am also dyslexic, I was fully supported and given ample time to complete tasks. Giving up was not on my options to do. I now felt more confident, associated with others better, able to control my worries and fears which was difficult for me before. I could communicate better and listen to others without any judgement. I had accepted my disability and I was making steady progress into continuing with my courses on a much higher level with a long-term goal for self-employment.

With my efforts to keep calm and carry on and support from my tutor and fellow students, as I was able to be open at every stage of my condition. I certainly wouldn't be who I am today if I had given up. I have found renewed passion to help and inspire others by working to create online courses to support others. I am forever grateful for this opportunity and would strongly recommend anyone undergoing a challenge such as mine to consider learning opportunities like this as it has been positively life changing.

I was uplifted and felt really valued beyond measure to read a statement from my nominator about my learning journey and how it all began. I had never thought that someone was even paying attention and monitoring my attendance and progress. The amount of determination and courage, despite all I was undergoing, was reflected in that same statement.

I enrolled on a counselling course in April 2018 and successfully completed the ten week course gaining a Level One Award in Counselling Skills. In September 2018, I made the decision to continue my counselling studies journey and commenced a Level Two Counselling Course, completing a Certificate in Counselling Skills in March 2019. I had also completed other training at RFLD, namely an award in sewing skills, Sewing for Enterprise, Complementary Therapy and Business Planning and Enterprise.

I am planning to continue my counselling studies as a means of equipping myself with sufficient knowledge and skills in my new career path to help and impact many lives through sharing my experience whilst coaching and holding workshops.

My nominator continued to say that I was an inspiration to my colleagues, and family and friends. Also by the way, I had changed during the course. They felt that I was calmer and was accepting of my life challenges. They also felt that I was a great listener and was not judgemental

My nominator was asked about why I deserved a Suffolk Adult Learning Award? The nominator was able to provide what was remarkable about the impact of my learning achievements on me, and also where relevant, on my family, friends, and my community. This included some of the challenges I had overcome and how I did it, and how I could motivate and inspire others to learn.

"What is remarkable about Josephine is that she has been able to open up her thinking to consider a change in career path when faced with a life changing injury. Josephine was on the verge of starting a rewarding and physically active career before her injury occurred. Being faced with limited mobility, Josephine sought out opportunities to change her deteriorating mental health and well-being by exploring training opportunities. She has a diagnosis of Complex Regional Pain Syndrome affecting her foot and ankle as well as a medically unexplained condition of right leg pain, major anxiety, PTSD, and clinical depression. She is reliant on crutches to remain mobile.

The impact the training has had on Josephine has helped her to build back her self-confidence, improve her mental well-being and be fully available for her young child. She feels it has helped her to achieve a level of normality in which her coping skills are expanding. Josephine has been an inspiration to her fellow students, and she has been able to assist another learner to further develop study skills and would always go the 'extra mile' in participating in class discussions and skills practice even when in extreme discomfort.

Alongside her studies and parenting responsibilities, Josephine also volunteers at her local church and is an ambassador for the Prince Wako Foundation in Uganda. She is keen to ensure that young girls gain the support and resources needed to remain in education and gain qualifications."

Do not be side-tracked by people
who are not even on track.

By this I mean you have the power and responsibility to do whatever it takes to not be blown off track by any kind of wind. Try your hardest not to engage in every battle that comes your way. It should stick into your mind that if the battle is not between you and your destiny, it is simply a distraction. The majority of people, including me, have fallen into this trap time and time again but we all learn in the end. We often want to try pleasing other personalities, especially friends or family members because according to some myths, it is a taboo to let any of them down. This kind of character and attitude or behaviour can easily lead to the killing of dreams, confidence, vision, or goal for someone who does it for the sake of comforting someone else. This approach can never lead you to reaching the bright shining stars that you have always wished yourself to achieve.

It gets to the point where you cannot do it anymore. You have to be firm and bold to decide not to be side-tracked by those individuals who are not on track. Retrain your brain to change your mindset and acknowledge that you have to ignore some kind of negativity that comes along the way of your situation. You could be favouring someone, stand by them but they have a different goal from yours. At times, and I cannot emphasise this enough, communication and listening skills are key if you want to be fully informed and analyse each scenario situation.

Siding with someone because you are scared of how people will perceive you if you did not will destroy your core source of joy, peace and happiness. What you should be aware of is that other people not taking any of this behaviour are out there, living the time of their lives and you are not. Think twice and know that you are brave and stronger than you think if you explore this side of you, stop living for other people and be yourself. I want you to know that if you are simply scared of being hated, although it sounds louder than noise, you should also know and remember that love and self-care are more fulfilling than you ever imagined and this is me talking from personal experience.

Until I decided that this did not satisfy me, I was brutally hurting, could not stop crying, was miserable and my confidence hit rock bottom. I felt unworthy, never felt motivated or inspired anymore and it was definitely not healthy for my well-being and a few of those people around me who truly cared. This I would never wish either to sit back and relax without creating an awareness that could save you or anyone you know from undergoing this route.

Don't worry about being branded by certain names for being yourself because at the end of the day, you want to liberate and identify who you truly are and to establish that inner pure joy and happiness from within which will lead you to define your purpose of existence. By sticking to this approach, my life feels brand new and I would wish you, or someone you know to experience it too.

It is of paramount importance that you avoid drama and negative people as it is so refreshing. Remove yourself from anything or anyone you feel is draining you and watch your life improve. I know you may be having mixed feelings and emotions about this life of yours and how you get to the point where you can make the decision on how you would like to live it. However much I felt this way too, I had to be assertive and erase some memories to be able to move on. I did not have to forget how a particular individual meant to me but I accepted that they were not that person anymore.

I knew I was not created to be used but created to be valued, respected and to be a success so I stopped allowing people to use me, knew my worth and how incredible I was which implies that it all starts with you.

CHAPTER THREE

The Power And Glory Of God

I somehow came to realise that no matter what was against me, I did not have to mind it. I always kept in mind that God is all around me and in my way, that he will always be there to protect me. I established that at such times even if I felt like my challenges overshadowed my Christianity. I however, was speaking to people who were empathetic and believed in God and because they knew me and how I had always been a believer, they never gave up on me and each time they would either talk to me about old memories, something they thought that could excite me, ask me something not relating to my situation and other times when things appeared intense to even talk about anything, I would be crying endlessly and they allowed that. Having friends and family that stick by you in times like this are so rare, so you should always keep an eye on them and never let them go or take them for granted.

I am someone who always wants to wear a smile despite anything, but it got to a point where my smile was ugly, worthless and awful. Without mentioning names here, there were those key people who use to call and say, 'let's pray,' or if they called and knew that there would be no other way of getting through to me they would just call on the Holy Spirit to lead us in this prayer and for some reason each time someone talked about God or quote scriptures in the bible, I would intuitively listen and my heart would calm down and would get into it. I would say thank you for their quality time and lifting me spiritually and like my Mum has always said, read the bible, continuously say prayers, open your heart, ask for forgiveness and forgive too. These words I have always kept close as my ringtones despite anything else I am undergoing.

I know how easy it is not to identify the power of God, to be overshadowed and also, although you may have friends and family or other medical experts and take various medications, I found that none of this was useful without having an open heart and having God in your life. I have spoken to a few people and I also know those who are really struggling and suffering with pain, frustration and trauma and much more but pretend to be okay. This is extremely damaging and others seem to react to your situation but deep down knowing what they are going through, they feel embarrassed or ashamed to disclose anything. Although the reason for what you are going through is not the same as mine, this has to be confronted and brought to the surface before God. You may not have to tell anyone else but God knows you and what you are going through. I identified that the more tears and anger I had, there's no one who would understand it, no one I could speak to in detail. I hated to be living in denial and having a bleeding heart full of bitterness due to my situation.

You should also note that some people in your circle may want to pretend to be there for you but in the actual sense, they would be spying on you, mocking you, talking about you behind your back or even wishing that you stay in the same situation as some may feel you are a threat to them. And all this is revealed through reading the bible, understanding the words, and opening your heart.

I constantly asked the Holy Spirit to lead me and always referred to reading Ephesians chapters one and two for a deeper understanding. I had to pray. Whilst fasting, I opened my heart, body and soul, and believed in his word. I also cried a lot during all this. I could listen to his voice. I prayed for divine revelations through a vision of a dream. It was revealed to me by God's grace that I was saved through faith. I cannot say that the result was my own effort but God's gift, so I cannot boast about it. God was to manifest himself to me through dreams and most times I could understand and interpret the dreams or ask someone who knew better and more and they would clarify things for me which made sense and through this process, I never stopped praying. I could go to bed calling on the Holy Spirit to be with me whilst praying for others too. You too should never take dreams for granted.

Whilst undergoing all this, I drew myself to God closely because I knew that when I went to sleep, even only for two or three hours, I received a clear message from him that helped to reposition me. At some point this felt so unreal and it freaked me out but I knew God had my back and had to trust and believe in him to lead me wherever he would want me to go. This is something one has to be attentive to because in most cases, we want to see miracles but we don't want to be in a situation for them to be manifested. I had to be certain of what I was allowing to define me by looking to God and his strength and seek his face as indicated in 1 Chronicles 16:11. I started to firmly acknowledge that however much I was undergoing and battling with, only God who gave me life can give me identity and healing.

I have identified how powerful God is and I am positive and hopeful and each time I get these negative thoughts and voices, whether something discouraging or trying to hinder my breakthrough, I know how to tackle with a tailored prayer. The book of Psalms in the bible became my best friend and I rarely skipped a day without reading psalms 23 'The Lord is My Shepherd.' This was so relieving and therapeutic for me.

I wanted to do better and overcome all that I have had to deal with, feel better and make steady progress as I was feeling so uncomfortable as I knew I had a vision and purpose for my future and this condition had been limiting me to unlock my potential. I know it is very hard to pull through and it needs courage, hard work, perseverance, belief and the need to have faith. Some of the words I constantly spoke over and again in my life:

Holy Spirit here I am.

Reveal to me your power because I know if I do not have the Holy Spirit.

I cannot be delivered.

Holy Spirit transform me.

Change me.

Heal me.

Answer me.

Forgive me.

I accept you Holy Spirit to do your work in me.

Holy Spirit you are smart.

May my heart receive a new song of gratitude, joy, happiness and fulfilment.

Please fill me with divine revelation.

Make me a minister of fire.

Baptise me with your Holy Spirit and fire.

Thank you for freely giving me your protection, fighting my battles, challenges, healing and delivering me, disarming all powers of the enemy.

Holy Spirit be my best friend.

The fear of being scared is not worth it.

The power of God has enabled me to attract people who would help me identify my purpose and have good Samaritans at the same time. You see, when you become intimate with God you will be overwhelmed with his ways and you can actually have a conversation with him and he will respond back with an action, message through his chosen messengers, or a dream revelation. I found out that every time I needed anything to be done or receive something I would just say it and it was done.

As I struggled to bend or reach for things, one person who used to support me got a revelation that they had to organise people to come to my house and clean it from top to bottom. Five of them helped without charging me anything and afterwards they prayed with me and made a remark that God loves me and He was healing me. I was covered in goose bumps because I had been contemplating on how my house would be cleaned and how I would manage doing it. But guess what, God was there making it all happen for me.

I know you too may have or had days whereby you woke up feeling fed up and tired and feeling like, 'what's the point,' and crying so loudly asking why you and what ifs and spend the whole day in bed. But a couple of times this happened to me someone would either call me and talk over things in my life, visit me or bring me something that I did need without mentioning it to them and for me, those signs enabled a gradual step by step road to breaking through with the power of God that I just couldn't keep to myself but share it.

Whatever the case maybe dear one, I just want to reassure you that don't ever let anyone intimidate you, dismiss you, minimise you or define you. God is with you, loves you and delights in you and for you. Whether you think you are not worthy, a big sinner and think God can only speak to certain people, this is a lie. But if only you can commit to know and understand him, he will take you the way you are from zero to HERO, just like he has done for me.

Please do not perish because of lack of information and knowledge because any evil spirit power and darkness of the challenge you are undergoing could attract you to an uncomfortable situation. Know how to glorify in the power of God by testifying, praising, sharing great news, and being thankful. All this overpowers the devil and forces him to bow down and die.

CHAPTER FOUR

Losing A Dream Job

Having worked in so many other places like you may have done too or lost a job for some reason or a contract came to an end or you were made redundant, I am sure that you can compare which kind of job you preferred the most. I have nothing against anywhere else I worked but this was the job for me and I called it my 'BEST FIT'.

This began from the interview process where I felt so relaxed and I was able to ask all that I needed to know and they were able to clarify my queries which hit the spot I needed. Although this was far from where I lived (Ipswich to Chelmsford) on a daily basis, this was never a limiting block for me. I was happy.

I started in February and had the injury towards the end of April. I remember I was fully supported and valued. I believe this was due to my ability to be keen to learn and ask questions where I was not sure - in short, I was true to myself. I remember having a few errors when my work was audited in the second week, and then this also happened in the third week. My manager invited me for a catch up and she mentioned this and I openly disclosed my biggest concerns with her. I thought I would be told that this was not the job for me but I was comfortable in saying what the problem was. Surprisingly, she had already noticed but did not know how she could put it across to me without me mentioning it first; that being, my dyslexia. The moment she knew, more support was organised for me which I had not expected and from this point, I knew I was wanted on the team. I was okay to share my condition with other team mates who had not even noticed that I was battling to mention it as I was new on the team. My sense of humour and personality, communication and ability to go the extra mile in all my work shone through. My job was my second home and family and I remember what I was called every time I received a phone call or I came into the office and that was, 'Hello Sunshine'

Anyways, I was getting on in the job really well and was planning to move closer to work. My injury happened on a Friday but again on the same day I had a review and they said they were proud of my work and they were going to confirm to me on Monday about a permanent position.

Throughout my injury, although the job role was not extended due to my illness and inability to work or drive there, I kept in touch and updated my employer every single detail of my progress, and from April to August that year, given the fact that I was not a permanent employee, I was treated so well even though at the time I felt that I had been betrayed or let down as I could not get to work owing to something that was never my fault. Looking back now, if they had not made that decision, I would still be fighting to now cope with my disability as a result. They had foreseen this before I did.

What I am trying to emphasise here is that we should always be open and always do our best when given the opportunity within any work setting. This thought process could also be transferred to your personal life, helping others or by doing a voluntary role. The time you share and how you express this brings remarkable memories that you will be proud of and cherish during a healing process. Let's not always be quick to judge or complain about a certain situation that has happened by blaming others because when you actually see the light you can be grateful and acknowledge the reason why that decision was made. I had this same feeling about my employer ending my contract but little did I know at the time that my injuries would last to this point. We all should always think before we speak or create a negative mind that could be detrimental to those around us or in our own lives.

However traumatic and upsetting this experience was for me and to reflect and talk about the thing that happened to me that changed everything about my style of life wasn't easy. As part of my healing therapy and with unstoppable and endless tears rolling down my cheeks, I believed it was time to face the lion and air it all out. I am confident that the next time you happen to be in any public environment like I was, you will be aware and be careful whilst being mindful of what could happen to you. I know this because I was caught unaware too. What happened to me I would never wish it for anyone else because it was terrible beyond measure!

For me, saving a life is more rewarding than keeping it all to myself. I cannot watch another life suffer unexpectedly through being silent. Nearly all of us go shopping at some point but none of us expect to experience the injury and pain that I suffered by doing so. Although personally I still experience a peak of phobia at going shopping or to the extent of even imagining it, I know I shall overcome it but with one step at a time.

CHAPTER FIVE

The Power Of Talking

Amidst everything that was happening in my life, I recall being tired and fed up with everything you could ever think about. I was in pain, my mobility was poor, and everywhere I went in terms of hoping to get an answer or solution got me referred to someone else. I had had enough of that. I felt rejected and disrespected. I wanted to be out of this dark shell that I felt trapped in. It was a tough decision but I knew if I didn't, who would have done it for me? I had looked on YouTube and all other social media outlets to seek help. However much I did this I felt like exploding! I needed to be heard by someone who embraced empathy.

Guess what? I identified that I was kind of thinking that I had control over everything that I was undergoing. I dealt with my situation with so much anger, frustration, and hate, which was not getting me anywhere. I came to realise this when I undertook some cognitive behaviour therapy (CBT) sessions that I found helpful. I was able to explore various triggers of specific episodes of my worst moments where I felt that I needed to find out more. I was attending these sessions on a weekly basis however, something was missing. I also tried connecting with other people who had tried this CBT counselling to see if it was working for them but found that there were more who felt more like I did. This created curiosity that enabled me to look deeper within me. I wrote down a few things that I needed clarity on and why I was feeling this way. I needed to investigate it further to enable me tackle it by taking action.

I mean the question was, therapists usually offer up to twelve sessions of CBT and clients would feel a difference but how could it be the opposite for me? I had over twenty sessions and it got to a point where they could not help me anymore. I was unable to discuss how I felt and my concerns about why I felt there was no progress because each time I attended the appointment, it felt like my first one. This was alarming but I never wanted to give up and leave it like that. I realised that I needed to look around for more information about this and the more I dug deeper the more I found out that at the point where I was at, most people had either given up on the sessions or had major suicidal thoughts. For those who were still surviving, some could not seek out more help as they felt that they were not being heard or understood, especially if English was not their first language.

I identified that it was a big problem as people were feeling ashamed to disclose everything about themselves. I was in pain and affected by all these symptoms but I knew I just could not allow this to happen to anyone else who had suffered like the way I had or the other people I had spoken to. For me, this was very healing and called for me to take action and allow the mighty doors of opportunity to open for me.

I remember a time when nothing made sense to me anymore. The degree at which betrayal portrayed itself in a number of incidences in my life felt unbearable but deep down I knew that if I didn't pick myself up, who the HELL would? Was this the kind of standard I wanted? Had I completely failed? Is there anything else I could do to improve myself? I asked myself these questions out loud. I knew that even though I went to the doctors or other experts, no one could have understood as much as I did other than me. I recorded my thoughts and listened back to them but still this was not intuitively me. Everything else was a struggle and from this, my plan was born.

You may already be aware that the world is not as bad as some people think neither are the people in it. There are some really incredible people out there and I just had to find them. You see, this is what happens if you are a Christian, have faith and believe in God. Well to me, that's what I found. I started asking God specific answers which I witnessed myself through the results of exactly what I had prayed for. I felt I had the seeds of greatness and an abundance of spirituality to be a generational blessing which required me to distance myself from situations and people who tried to steer me away from my destiny to rise over and above. I connected with people who I was able to open up to with brief disclosure and some of them had noticed my situation and were concerned to help selflessly. This was soothing, healing and felt comfortable. Never had there been a point whereby I was pressured to give feedback to them, but they were there, comforting and reassuring me. Also, having undertaken a course in counselling and listening skills, and acting out various scenarios during the practical assessments of these role plays as counsellor, client, and observer, I was personally making it my own and via this, feedback was provided. This played a massive role in overcoming every negative thought and bad experience that I was encountering. It was painless, free and therapeutic because I was talking to people who accepted me, congruent and empathetic.

You may be in doubt or fear of whatever you are undergoing through because of a dysfunctional situation you are unable to cope with or manage. Trust me, I do understand and get it but what you need to do is to find people who have what you need and talk to them and this will shake off any doubts and excuses to enable you determine your destiny. It is important to know that people don't have power over you, but you give it to them. You have to learn to take your power back. This takes someone who is strong and determined. As for me, I knew I could never have moved forward without being in an unstable environment. It was either stay in the same situation and keep beating myself over it or work my way out of it.

Through talking, I was able to understand my situation better, clarify the queries that I had, and enable me to make better decisions on top of securing long lasting genuine relationships from those who cared and were supportive in my best interests.

Services available whilst encountering tough situations.

One may wonder why other services may not be involved at this point. Life is not as straightforward as we think it would be in everyone's life. It got to a point where specific individuals I would have counted on in the past turned their backs away in so many unspeakable ways. To clarify on this here, I just want to reassure you that if you have ever had any kind of doubt within you that all that glitters is GOLD, then no it isn't. I really had to undergo this situation to have a clear understanding of the kind of environment I was surrounded by without any kind of judgement. It is when I was at my lowest when I identified how many people would actually stand by me, encourage me, brighten my day, pray for me or with me, reassure me that everything would be okay as opposed to being talked about behind my back, who lied and laughed about me, celebrated my loss, pain and suffering, behaved a certain way and treated me differently, hid away each time they got in contact, feeling embarrassed or ashamed to call me their friend or family and were happy to ignore me.

Your widely open jaw may be dropping from your chin right now to your chest, which is understandable but such is life. Until you are in such a challenging situation, you will never know who is who on the surface. Now that I have been there and in the recovery process, a part of my call to action plan, I am super grateful of what happened to me and the period this has taken me to acknowledge my power which I am confident has qualified me to be able to influence others by motivating and inspiring others who are finding it extremely challenging to deal with it.

This was eye-opening and brought so much tears that cleansed away the extreme pain, frustration, anger, and the feeling of being undervalued but after all this, there was calm. I reflected on Jeremiah (1:8-10) where I understood that I did not need to be afraid and sad anymore because God was with me. He reached out his hand and touched my mouth and said to me, 'I am putting words into your mouth and today I have put you in charge of nations and kingdoms that I would pull up and tear down, destroy and overthrow, build up and plant." I was able to draw myself closer to God and let go of all that I had undergone through and start to work on the power of forgiveness to be free. However hurtful and disappointing this was, I sat down and thought deeper from within of the damage this had created but on the other side, I knew that unless someone is walking the same way as you are, you must never deviate anyone from their own route journeys if they do not have it within them.

Some may pretend but the truth about them will always stay and can reflect somewhere, somehow, and anytime. We all just have to pay attention not to be entirely overtaken by anything we are aware of and doubted. When it comes to reality, it's just a matter of time. And the reasons can resurface. Never be quick to react or blame yourself for other people's inconsistency to support and help you out.

Life is full of experiences and surprises but I had to stay true to who I was and still am. Never fight or abuse or accuse someone even when being provoked to do so. Here you are at peace with yourself and can never regret what you would have responded back to. My situation enabled me to pick myself up with a strong armour, become bold and be fully aware that it was my responsibility if I wanted anything else to change in my life and be able to support my son in the best way possible. I had so many ideas, decisions to make and how I would make a start on each but had no choice, but as a Christian, I called on the Holy Spirit to lead me and show me the way, to be understood and find a way where there seemed to be none. Everything I had encountered was planned by God, oven baked, and nurtured in order to identify my calling which is why I would never have been able to share my experience without undergoing it. Looking back and reflecting, I am so grateful it happened and for God to manifest himself to me.

i. **GP, Private Care, Pain Management**

It had got to the point where I had enough. It felt to me that I had taken the medication as I was prescribed and the best I was getting from the medical professionals was to either up my dosage or refer me to another doctor and from another doctor to another specialist etc.

"Josephine," I recall one specialist saying, "you are suffering with chronic pain with symptoms of complex pain regional syndrome so it's not that you will be getting better."

So with this, I was introduced to undertaking sessions of understanding and living with chronic pain. Although I found the content helpful and useful, I was unable to implement any of the techniques or approaches due to the severe pain. I remember asking a couple of specialists that if nothing else could be done for me, I wanted to be referred for my leg to be cut off. In my mind, I did not know how else to articulate my pain and symptoms or that I preferred to having just one leg rather than the pain. Little did I know that had they complied with my request, I would still have continued to suffer with my lower back and lumbar which had resulted in my spine to twist. I had been to the doctors and due to my severe pain, even the physiotherapists did not want to touch my leg and foot as they did not want to aggravate the pain. So it was one morning when I asked to view my medical report and the medication I was on, I must admit, it takes guts to do so.

I had a confrontational conversation with the G.P and other experts about my report and I asked kindly to be listened to as opposed to someone just assuming what is wrong with me after a very long time and suggesting how to best approach my situation and medication as well. I found that doctors have so much to do and research plus lots of clients to see and at times they are thinking about the next patient. Following my appointment I was given a platform each time which was not 100% there but I got better treatment and time with the way I was handled too. This made a huge difference to my healing process. Never be shy or feel stuck to speak up and give a genuine explanation of your signs and symptoms of your illness.

ii. **PTSD, Depression, and Anxiety**

Major concerns here were about how I felt I was not being perceived correctly. I had so many things I was dealing with such as the signs and symptoms of the strong medication I was on.

I remember at times when the taxi that I used to use to pick up or drop my son at school would arrive and I was still sleeping. I was made to pay waiting charges each time. I struggled financially and I remember relying on food bank parcels. I was gaining a lot of weight which was making me uncomfortable and hardly had anything to wear apart from the two or three dresses that I could still fit in to.

Most times I did not know whether I was coming or going and although my smile always covered everything up, I was internally bleeding. I wanted to be pain free but the side effects were too much. I would sometimes throw up sick full of blood and my bowel movements were blood as well. It was worrying and scary and I felt so weak. I grew bad thoughts to make everything go away but I believe if you have ever suffered from any or all of these mental health issues yourself, you would know what I mean.

Some G.Ps and other medical experts kept referring to my mental health but this was not the main issue, which I feel I must address here.

Due to the level of mental health concerns within this country, especially around my community, everyone has one or two things that could trigger their mental illness, and as a result of visiting the doctors, more antidepressants will be prescribed again and this comes along with so many side effects that can be detrimental. In this case, I started reading around the symptoms and signs and provided feedback. This can help to improve your situation by being on the right medication and be able to identify an improvement. And again, providing feedback to those people whose first language is not English and struggle expressing themselves and end up not doing any research, hence agreeing with the medical expert 100%.

If I had not done this, I would not be where I am today. So if you have to write down any queries about your health before visiting the G.P, just do so and to take along someone with you who is aware of your situation to avoid dying silently or being traumatised without having any voice. In my situation, my main concern was aimed at the symptoms as opposed to the root cause which was not right. From this point, it is rather unfortunate that I noticed how people can give up by ending their lives as they feel they are in the middle of nowhere and due to their anxieties, lose hope of being helped.

iii. **School**

If you are a responsible and caring parent, you would know how much effort you have to put in to pick up and drop off kids at school on a daily basis and everything else that comes with it. During my hardest times I felt that I could not cope or do this anymore. A few people who could have helped had other obligations and did not even live close to where I did. This was challenging for me despite all the other struggles I was encountering. What changed was when one day when I went to pick up my son, I was asked how I was by a teacher. I was in so much pain, limping, fed up, on crutches and frustrated and I remember being invited into the office. I was past being ashamed and have to admit, I broke down crying. The head teacher and her deputy were so concerned and took the time to listen to me. Although they knew I had been struggling, they were oblivious to how serious my situation was and to how much of it I was keeping to myself. Here, in front of both of them, I was able to unburden myself.

Both the head teacher and her deputy were so understanding and asked how they could best support me. I explained all my issues and they ensured me that they would help in whichever way they could so that I was happy, and that every now and then they would check up on me. I explained that it was also hard to support my son with his homework and they were able to help out and support him during his after school club which helped to relieve some of the tension I had.

I could have made the decision to keep this all to myself but I wouldn't have been able to be supported or signposted to other various services such as bringing in the family practitioner who was able to work with the school and my son with emotional a well-being. He was introduced to other young carers and so could associate himself with other kids whose parents were in the same situation. I was also allocated a social worker who identified the kind of help I needed for home caring and arranged for a charity organisation to give some of their time to visit me at home each week for reassurance and hope. No way would I have been able to come through this without any help and I believe that you may be in doubt whilst struggling with any challenge you may be dealing with. Just be rest assured that you don't have to deal with it alone for if you open up, you will be signposted to where you will be best supported.

CHAPTER SIX

Imaginary Place

You might be wondering what an imaginary or comfort place is here and what it has got to do with my breakthrough. If you have struggled and suffered or are still in the same chronic situation you will love this. However tough life has been since the injury I thought I could continue being a superwoman who could manage anything at any time. Well, in 2017 and 2018 I managed to travel to Uganda where most of my entire family live. It was extremely difficult for me to travel but I got help from the airport both ways.

Well my financial situation in the 2019 summer holiday was really bad and we just managed to survive. Having had Christian's Against Poverty (CAP) helping me to manage my debts, the only option foreseen was to go bankrupt which I did not want to consider. I mean the advantage of being debt free seemed like a reward but how favourable are the results when the majority of the current privileges are waived? In addition to this, if I was to invite one of my family members from back home, this would have raised the question as to whether I had needed to be declared bankrupt in the first place and whether such a reunion would scupper any bankruptcy application.

Despite any challenges you may be undergoing, especially the financial side of things, you must always ensure that you know the consequences. I was so worried and scared about this so I asked if I could have a couple of months to think over things and if this was the way path I really wanted to take. Never be quick to make a decision just because it seems the quickest way out. So having considered all the possible solutions, for me, none of them would work out.

Every parent during summer time does amazing activities with their kids, visiting family, flying away, and so much. For my case this was not possible. With my mobility being limited and in severe pain with some bone dislocation, I could get stuck at any time. I could not afford this so I thought of something else to resolve my predicament.

You know, if you are like me or maybe know someone like me who loves travelling, taking pictures, enjoys therapeutic therapies like massage, aromatherapy or reflexology and enjoys sipping on a lovely non-alcoholic pina colada drink, my heart, body and soul melts at the thought of being in this kind of exotic place. If like me you find this impossible, try putting on some exotic music, close your eyes and take yourself to an imaginary place where you can visualise yourself on a tropical beach and raising your hand up for beach service. Look up at the cloudless blue skies and imagine all your cares just melting away. To make the most of this moment to the fullest, try your hardest to block out anything else that could stop you from focussing and enjoying your holiday adventure in your imaginary place. I introduced this to my seven year old son who absolutely swears by it and loves it too. He understood our financial struggle and why we could not travel anywhere that year. Although he was aware of this, I had to try and explain it again as most of his friends had been away and he had not. I reassured him and praised him for how special he was and how things would get better. This approach saved me a lot of money and I urge that if you are struggling the same way, you should definitely consider trying it out for you and yours.

Never compare yourself to others.

If you have or are still dealing with a disability, mental health or any other kind of illness like me, you should stop comparing yourself to other people. If you find yourself doing this then stop and put yourself back on the right track.

I still remember the times when I was so unwell but continued to carry myself as though I was ok. I kept posting pictures and writing up motivating and inspiring messages on Facebook and WhatsApp where a good number of people commented, liked, wowed, and also asked an increasing number of engaging questions. They also complimented me and I appreciated the comments about what those people loved about me and how I looked. I pretended I was normal and that everything was okay but although this was not me at all, I kept comparing myself to other people who were doing the same thing as I was.

I never wanted to give any indication that I was melting, dying, had lost it, was bleeding, screaming or anything else you would want to call the feelings and emotions I was experiencing. You see, so many people are just putting up an appearance because someone else is doing it. I know so many people who have reached out to me to ask how I managed to cope and was always smiling and looking content. Amidst all I had to deal with, I was capable of holding myself up and advise them on how I did this. Once we had built up a relationship, I would share my number with them and tell them that I would be there for them each time they needed to talk or unleash any challenging situation they encountered. I would do my make up and put a wig on o as to look strong which I always managed to pull off but, immediately after each call I would cry so loud, my wig would turn into a makeup remover and then I'd throw it down. I hated myself for this charade and how I was managing to do it but again, people started to make changes in their lives because of this and this feedback was uplifting to some extent.

I realised that the more I played this character the more damage I created for myself and the harder it got to deal with. But I also recall that sometimes when my friends called I would pretend to be busy with something and would call them back, that is if I even I picked up in the first place, or I would pick up and shout at them and say I did not want to talk. One friend in particular noticed this and asked me why I did not want to talk but still my response was that I just did not want to talk and hung up. Trust me, there are so many in this category. If you are not one of them, at least you may know someone who is either from your own family or a close friend. The most important thing here is not to point fingers. Here, I am aiming for you to be congruent and accept that this is so real and damaging.

Let not the circumstances you are dealing with be overshadowed by not staying in your lane because it causes more damage. The situation you are in will not be forever, and it may be happening for a reason. In my case it has shaped me into a stronger person and being true to myself I have been inspired to write about it for awareness purposes. Do not cover your scars with various toxic layers. Choose to be you and those who would resonate with you will stay till the end of time and it will stop you from hurting as well as bleeding internally. I know how this tortures to the core bone. It is deadly!

In my situation, I was unable to perform in the normal job that I had; I couldn't embrace it and it was killing me. What with this, the constant pain, and struggling financially, my concentration or ability to grasp anything anybody said to me was a nightmare. Those I used to work with were either getting keys for their new house or car, or had started their master's degree or had been promoted, all of which I felt I deserved too. Even though I wished all those things for myself, I could not achieve any of them in my situation hence I accepted that I had to stay in my lane. Nevertheless, I encouraged myself with the fact that this situation was not forever. So, I picked myself and vowed not compare myself to anyone else other than myself and I pray that you do the same because it has worked so perfectly for me.

How I found purpose by helping a girl through Children in Need (Interview - August 2018).

I am a self-motivated individual with a vast knowledge in food and nutrition, and complementary therapy alternatives. My actions and words exhibit my love for my motherland

Uganda, Africa, and the less privileged girl child. My passion for humanity has driven me towards developing several soft skills, being certified in counselling and listening skills with a background in business and human resource management. In April 2017, I sustained a life changing body injury that streamlined my direction and the things I prioritized in life. With physical injury came a limit to the things I could do. As I struggled to heal myself, I chose to be part of a cause that could heal the rest of the world. I sat down with a team who were intrigued to discuss my passion which was the Prince Wako Foundation. and I learned properly about how to use my personal experiences to contribute to healing the world.

1. **"Josephine. How did you get involved with the Prince Wako Foundation?"**
   "That is quite interesting. Well I was talking to Joshua Wako who was already running projects under the foundation. He shared his vision, what he does and all that he had done previously. He also talked about the girl children in need and what kind of efforts had been employed to meet those different needs. This prompted me to ask a couple of questions about the vision and what pushed him to do what he did and the kind of things he did daily to make sure the girl child in need receives help. His reply was quite inviting. He gave me time to think about it and asked me to give my thoughts

on the presented vision at an opportune time. At that time, I was at one of the lowest moments in my life, but when I scrolled through the foundation website, I was touched. There and then I chose to get involved."

2. **"Have you ever started any other Prince Wako project from scratch. If so, tell us about it?"**
   "Personally, I came in at a time when there was a need for volunteers and ambassadors to provide a voice to the girl children in need. So, the concluded charity projects were my first."

3. **"In your experiences so far, what have been the challenges?"**
   "In my experience, the scarcity of resources has been a challenging factor. In recent projects, I visited two schools, Verona High School, Mutundwe-Uganda, and St. Andrews Primary School in Jinja. There are several children that are in need and there are only a few people that can raise funds. This goes to say that we practically need the support of people who can raise funds to be used to cater for the needs of these children. Basically, there is a higher demand of needs amongst the children and yet the resources are limited."

4. **"Do you enjoy working for the girl children? What inspires you?"**
The absolute truth, from the bottom of my heart, is that I really enjoy working for the girl children and actively taking part in the girl child help projects with the Prince Wako foundation explains it all. My inspiration is drawn from interacting with other girls. Having grown through all experiences like any other girl, I have learnt that I am surely privileged. I have been hit with the fact that these girls face tough times every day, and circumstances around them make them less privileged than I was when I was their age. The other day, when I visited the two schools, I interviewed a few and some of the things that did come up were that some students cannot stay in school because none of their parents can afford the required school fees. and others were HIV positive. Some are total orphans, and some are assaulted and sexually abused by their own step-fathers. The whole experience was so traumatizing. In some instances, girls who desperately wanted to stay in school had been forced to give in to sexual advances from different men so that they could raise their school fees. This for me is disheartening. No girl should go through this. There is a lot more to do. These girls are ambitious, they have goals and if we can deal with most of their insecurities,

things can turn around for the better. This inspires me every day, to see that they live a better life that leads them towards achieving their goals without trauma; this drives me."

5. **"What does volunteering for the Prince Wako Foundation involve?"**
"It involves so much. You get to meet like-minded people, people that are selfless, people with a common goal and vision. This comes with practical interactions with beneficiaries, actual on ground visits and thus transparency and accountability. In actual sense, we identify and work very closely with schools, communities and we know exactly how the funds raised are utilized. We get to interview beneficiaries, one after the other and based on circumstances, need and our vision, we prioritise accordingly. We also carry out group discussions to look for solutions and innovative ideas in different circumstances. Our work also involves inspiring, motivating, counselling, and creating awareness on a range of issues like the benefits of education, health tips, creativity, and personal development.

6. **"Describe your passion in relation to girl child empowerment. How do you think your passion impacts these young girl's lives in general?"**
"In recent projects, I shared with the girls my personal experiences. For example, where I studied for my O and A levels, where I went for my university education, my work experiences, the challenges that I have encountered all through and how I overcame them. Being an adult now, I know exactly what these children are going through. They can occasionally be taken up by circumstances and they may deviate from the rail of focus sometimes, but sharing with them one on one is so inspiring. They shared a lot more than they would have shared in a group. I shared my personal experiences with over 250 girls and I was so open with them. They were able to ask me any kind of questions. With overwhelming feedback, I realized that these girls felt comfortable, they knew how far they wanted to go with their studies, they believed in their potential and were ready to unlock it. Many started seeing life's realities in a broader perspective. From our talks, they got exposed to health issues within themselves and the need to say no to any kind of abuse at the right time. This being my passion, I was able to motivate and encourage them. With this impacting on them, they became happier even when they were a little tense in

the beginning. With an informal discussion, I believe that the experience created an everlasting impact and I am proud of it."

7. **"What is your vision for the entire organization. What are your main goals?"**
   "I like to see change, improvement, and I love to feel that these children in need, the very less privileged, and the abused move from one step in life to another. From having no support or feeling helpless to being focused on their studies, being creative and knowing that education is important to their growth and development. Well, it is important to note that when you educate a girl child, you educate a nation. When I interviewed some girls, I understood that they carried a lot of pressure from their homes which forces them into early sex practices. Their homes become arenas of intimidation. So, my main goal was to go forward with such noble campaigns, to find those that can support the cause and those that can raise funds to help support these children. I see most of these girls being moved away from the arms that put them in danger to safety. So far, the progress that I have seen in most beneficiaries is very promising. These girls should be strong, and they should not feel intimidated in any way.

8. **"What have been your favourite parts in your involvement in the different projects?"**
"Meeting and connecting with different kinds of people is so enriching, because we educate and inspire one another. With weekly meetings, creativity has made the whole experience so enjoyable. Having grown through a traumatic experience, the personal injury that I sustained, and the eventual healing process all have helped me to embrace my experience and see through most of these girl's eyes – there is a way where there seems to be no way. With my qualifications in business management and human resources, I have been able to actively get involved in the girl child help projects, which has helped me emotionally, psychologically and mentally to work with different passionate people. Thus, helping the girl child, easing some of their challenges also eases my health circumstances."

9. **What in your opinion needs to be done to empower the girl children?"**
"In my opinion, it is important to try and understand the girls. One should be able to fit in their shoes. As a certified counsellor, I know it is important to empathize with the person in the current situation and listen to them without judgement and blame. Even when many are getting involved in early and

risky sex practices, there is a need to understand the underlying cause. Therefore, we need to understand them and let them know that we are willing to work with them and find ways and enough funds to empower them. I think working well with the teachers is also significant. The teachers should be made aware of the circumstances surrounding the education of most of these children. As they educate them, they should attach value to their lives and the way they treat them. We as a people should be able to provide scholastic materials where need be, and essentials like sanitary pads and teach them how to use these pads. This will keep many in school. We should establish means of availing funds to cater for school fees so that these children go to school with no worries attached to financial requirements in school."

10. **"From your experience, which project do you think needs more effort?"**
    "We need to equip most of the teachers with skills to handle girls in crisis. There should be more efforts put in keeping the girl child in school. many lack the tuition fees, many do not have scholastic materials, many cannot access sanitary pads. If these issues are remedied, several will stay in school. Then health wise, there are several challenges, conditions, expe-

riences and diseases that need immediate intervention. Some have been sexually abused, others have abnormal and destructive menstrual cycles, and all these must be worked upon. We need more effort, financial backing and relevant counselling sessions with consistency."

11. **"Any words for anyone out there who wishes to support this cause?"**
    We are a small dedicated team that is growing time after time. Currently, we manage most of our own projects with the help of a few well-wishers. I call upon those who share a similar passion to join the cause. Efforts can be through monetary, material contributions or dedicating oneself to a service or skill for the cause. One can opt to avail oneself for a time in service of the cause. Anything with relevance can be of importance. If you want to be part of us, contact us and let us exchange ideas. Follow us on our media platforms, donate to the cause and fund a project that you may be personally interested in. With joint efforts focused on the girl child in need, the sky's the limit.

I knew that if I didn't make an effort to heal from what hurt me, I would continue to bleed on people who didn't cause my challenging situation. You can imagine how my seven year old son was feeling whilst I was undergoing this condition.

Despite all I was undergoing, I continually questioned myself silently. 'Josephine, have you fully healed from what hurt you or are you still bleeding on people who didn't cut you?' Well the honest answer was, I hadn't fully healed! I still had a lot of anger, hatred, unforgiveness, pain, frustration and much more, and it still resurfaces every now and then even now.

However, this is what I have learned. Getting frustrated and hurt may not have been my fault, but getting healed is 100% my responsibility. I now feel that it's not fair putting the burden of past failures and mistakes onto somebody else, especially those close to me or you. It's not fair to allow somebody else to pay for your pain. It's not fair bleeding on people who did not cut you. I mean, if they truly love you and care, they will immediately want to help care for your wound, clean it, bind it and soothe you until it heals, but if I keep taking off the bandage and picking on the wound, how long would I want them to them to keep helping me bind this wound?

You see, I noticed that my healing that was my responsibility. I had to decide to get healed for ME! I had to decide to get healed so I didn't have to keep bleeding on people who hadn't hurt me. I decided to get healed so others didn't continue to carry the burden of my past…it just wasn't fair on people.

One thing I have discovered about pain, PTSD and depression is that there is a root cause. I knew that something had happened and caused the situation I am suffering from but because it hadn't been dealt with properly. This wasn't bringing peace within. On the inside was aggravating major and severe symptoms of what I was dealing with.

I found that in as much as it is understandable and explains the challenges, does it excuse it however? NO, it just doesn't. Yes, you were hurt, betrayed, mistreated, injured, cheated on, accused of a crime you did not commit, abused, made feel worthless, and lied about. I do understand that explains how you feel and act, but does it justify it? NO, IT DOES NOT but healing is your responsibility.

I deliberately concentrated on ensuring that I would take responsibility for my healing to stop bleeding all over those who did not cut me. I believe that this could be ringing a bell for you, if so, just take it and say OUCH, and then start working on yourself.

CHAPTER SEVEN

How I De-Cluttered My Mind

I knew that it was easy for me to go around worried about my future, stressing over my finances, being frustrated over losing my job, tempted to live with guilt over what went wrong, past mistakes, and feeling bitter over what did not work out. I wondered why I did not enjoy life anymore, why I wasn't passionate about dreams and could not sleep well at night. This was because my mind was cluttered. I trust and believe that I was not created to live worried, frustrated, stuck, guilty, undervalued, disrespected, mistreated, feeling bitter, and upset, and if I was going to reach my destiny, I had to clear out the clutter.

I could not stop negative things from coming but I could stop them from staying. I did not have to hold on to them. When you make mistakes, guilt will come along with condemnation, telling us how we don't measure up, and if we hold on to it and be down about ourselves, we will either live our lives discouraged or we can let it go and say, 'Lord Father, thank you, for I am redeemed and thank you that I am forgiven. The past is over and this is a new day and I am moving forward.' When you go through disappointment and something doesn't work out, you cannot hold on to it or be discouraged; you must let it go. This is what I said. 'God, I know you have got something better, your plans for me are for good, I know you are directing my steps.' When the medical reports are not good, when you are in any challenging situation such as pain, being heartbroken, immobile, and depressed, you can either hold on to it, live your life being worried thinking, 'how am I going to get through this,' or you can let it go.

I had to meditate. I said, 'Lord, I know you are fighting my battles, I know that what's meant to harm me you are turning to my advantage. I may not see a way but God, I know you have a way.' You too can clear out the clutter, you can get rid of the negative things that are stuck killing your peace, taking your joy, and draining your energy. You have to be proactive when it comes to keeping your mind at peace. Throughout the day there will be noise, worry, and feelings of hate may surface but you don't have to hold on to them. Somehow living with worry has become normal to us and it's been done for years. Living with guilt is what we are used to.

We often feel that we don't deserve to be blessed. We have made so many mistakes or have been through a lot for so long that we have accepted it. We may be living with inferior feelings where someone is always telling us we are not that talented, smart, beautiful, or attractive. Due to this, we will never get better and because we do not know any better we accept it cluttering up our minds. You have enough people feeling negative about you and you don't have to do this to yourself as well. You have been made in the image of God the Almighty and he does not make any mistakes and you are his masterpiece.

Please do not say another negative word or thought about yourself. Quit dwelling on those people that are telling you what you are not because you are exactly how you are supposed to be; you have been wonderfully made. You should be playing this in your mind. 'I am a masterpiece, I am one of a kind, and talented. I am attractive, I am favoured, I am healed, I am empowered. I have the seeds of greatness that will automatically clear out the clutter.

'Fear can't stay where faith is; discouragement can't stay where hope is; guilt can't stay where forgiveness is, and mediocrity can't stay where greatness is. I just want you to programme your mind with what God says about you.

If you don't clear out your clutter, it will stop you from reaching a new level. Worry will keep you from rising higher, and feeling guilty will keep you from pursuing your dreams. Going around feeling offended and bitter will keep you from accessing new opportunities. Why did these people treat me this way, offend me, not help me? They did me wrong and that's why I am bitter and upset, but it happened ages ago. Why are you still holding on to it? Why are you still sour over the person who walked away? Still upset over how you were raised? Bitter over that company that let you go or someone who caused your injury? Do not poison your future, they hurt you once or twice but don't let them hurt you for the rest of your life.

Recognise that cluttering your mind is limiting your vision and I am not saying that what they did wasn't wrong or hurtful, and I am not making excuses for their behaviour, but as long as you are holding on to them, you are giving them your power and letting them control you. We only have so much emotional energy each day but do you know how much energy it takes to hold a grudge, to be bitter, and to go around trying to pay people back? That's valuable energy you need for your dreams, goals, and family. God said, he will give you beauty for ashes, but the key is, you have to let go of the ASHES before you receive the beauty after the space has been created.

Sometimes we feel that we have to get even and pay people back but this is not your responsibility, and if you turn this over to God, he will be your vindicator. He will bring justice into your life because he saw every hurt and wrong, every person that took advantage of you. I have learned that God will vindicate you better that you can. David said, 'God will prepare a table before you in the presence of your enemies.' This implies that when God brings you out, those people that did you wrong, the people that tried to hold you back will see you promoted and honoured in a position of influence. God will not vindicate for you in private but will do it in public. So your enemies will see you blessed, favoured, and successful.

So you may have plenty of good reasons to get upset, sad, depressed, worried, and not able to sleep at night but when you are in peace, that's a position of power and this shows God that you trust him not with your words but with actions too. The test comes when your contract has ended, medical reports are not good, could not do all you used to due to an illness or injury, or you are being provoked. Here is when clutter comes in but here is where God wants you to be still and trust him. You see the enemies' main target is our mind. As long as our mind is cluttered and filled with doubt, dwelling on such things as, what if I don't get better, find the right person, everyone hates me etc, then allowing these doubts to persist, you can never be clutter free and it keeps God from turning them around. When you face a big enemy, opposition to our God is bigger than any kind of illness or challenge. Do not talk about how big your problem is but how big God is. Just don't let fear clutter your mind or doubt to keep you from your miracles, and don't let people talk you out of your dreams.

The enemy will always try to defeat you first in your thoughts. Things like, you will never get better, do better, get over your addiction, forgive, or walk again. Don't believe those lies and God wouldn't be telling you that unless he knew it was on the way. Yes, your problem may be big but know the secret that God is much bigger, he has the final say and what he started in your life, he will finish. So when you are tempted to worry, turn it into worship and say, 'thank you so much that your angel's are working positively in your life. Thank you that no weapon that has formed against me will prosper. Thank you that the trap the enemy dug for me they will into it themselves.'

If we are to clear clutter in our lives, we need to know our responsibilities and God's role.

Sometimes we get frustrated because we are trying to do what only God can do. You can't make yourself get well or make someone do what's right. Our part is to believe, keep the faith, and let God do his part. Trust in him to work it out simply because there are some battles you are not meant to be involved in so you have to let God fight for you. But while waiting for things to change, this is a test to clear out your clutter and keep your mind on him. For example. 'God, thank you that you are in control. Thank you that your destiny for my life will come to pass. Thank you that you are for me.'

If we do our part, God will do his. He will not only keep you in peace but also get you to where you are supposed to be. When you can say I am going to stay in peace if it works out my way and I am going to stay in peace if it doesn't work out my way, then you take away all the power of the enemy. If you are only going to be happy if it works out your way then you are setting yourself up for disappointment. You can take a step by believing in God as he knows what's best for you, and it will allow him to do amazing things in your life.

Pay attention to what you are allowing into your spirit. Just because there is a conflict with your relatives doesn't mean it has to get in you. You could be frustrated about people playing politics, people not treating you right, or being in pain constantly. It is easy to sour your day and feel negative but you have to clear out that clutter. Your time is too valuable to live your life upset and bitter. This day is a gift from God and once we lose it, we can never get it back.

Sometimes we can get hooked on drama, trauma, worry, or fighting with family or friends, and forget to know what it is like to be in peace, but that is not the way God created us. You can choose to live from a place of peace; you don't have to let the outside get on the inside. Maybe you have become comfortable with the clutter and you don't realise that it is limiting your dreams and blocking your vision and potential. Not only that, it doesn't smell good. Worry doesn't look good on you. Guilt, jealousy, bitterness, feeling offended, anger, and stress. None of this is your style and the quicker you can get this clutter away you will step into new levels. Also be aware that you won't give birth to your dreams in a noisy place. That breakthrough you have been waiting for if you are worried and your mind is stressed won't give birth to your potential if your mind falls apart with hurt, regret and bitterness.

You may wonder why God is not doing anything. Perhaps he is waiting for you to find a quiet place. It may be noisy all around you but in your mind you can be in peace. When you know God is in control, directing every step, when you know nothing can stand against him, then you can live out of a quiet place. God is saying to you, 'come into the green pastures, come by the still waters, you don't have to carry all that clutter.'

It's time to get rid of the offence, guilt, regrets, anger, jealousy, and your negative mindset because there are some new things God wants you to birth. Promotions, dreams, breakthroughs, new contracts, healing, deliverance, restoration, and God is going to defeat enemies much better, open doors that you could not open and take you to the fullness of your destiny if you programme your mind positively.

I found out that the greatest enemy that was holding me back wasn't lurking somewhere outside of me. However much I did not want to accept, it is sad that my greatest enemy was right inside my head, in my mind, feeding me negative thoughts day in and day out. I could not run away from this enemy and certainly couldn't hide. But I chose to learn how to overcome those thoughts once and for all. Yes, I was hurt, broken, always being reminded, tired and exhausted, with so much anger and questions. Little did I know that there was no way to get to where I was created to be without going through this situation, and it was high time I embraced it by letting go in order to move on. I taught myself to be ready to be free from the endless inner battle of fighting my thoughts and chose to embrace a life of success.

In all personal challenges I came to witness that being poor is very simple; you can just choose to stay where you are. You can complain about everything and see opportunities pass you by therefore making a success of being poor. I was over hungry to break this chain, to get to where I was purposely created to be by embracing this course of action.

Never Ever Give Up On Yourself Even
When Others Have Done So To YOU.

CHAPTER EIGHT

The Golden Gift From GOD That I Could Not Afford to Disappoint Anymore.

JAYDEN. THE NAME MEANING, GOD HAS HEARD.

At the time when I had my injury my son had just turned five and he literally could tell you exactly how it happened and how he felt and still feels and the impact my situation had caused. My son is an intelligent, kind, honest and clever guardian angel who was there for me through thick and thin. Most times he would find me crying and grumpy and you could just see it through his eyes how torturing and traumatising it was for him too.

I was helpless and hated going out anywhere if it was not a must because walking was very tiring for me. I felt I could not fit in anywhere and having found and heard a few people talking about me behind my back who I never thought would do such a thing left me heartbroken and it was hard for me to accept. Dealing with the pain and my financial worries added to the problem. I felt that the best place and the safest option was to stay indoors nursing my wounds. I had to watch while my son trashed the entire place by throwing his toys everywhere, jumping from one chair to the other, and ripping the wallpaper off the walls. It was understandable as he was bored as he was not used to being kept indoors with no routine activities. It was sad but there was no other option to ease the situation as I was in a lot of pain myself.

So when I started to see the light at the end of the tunnel, I was more open and reassuring towards my son through talking. I contacted various services who were able to provide specialist health and well-being counselling for him that really helped whilst I was getting counselling as well. We were able to bond and have hard constructive conversations on my road to recovery.

My son constantly expressed how he felt about my situation. He could not concentrate at school as he was thinking about me and whether he would find me dead or alive! We said prayers on a daily basis and I recall him telling me how God was taking a long time to answer our prayers. I told him that it seems that when we say prayers we did not mean, we needed to focus more on what we prayed for and that God was taking his time. I encouraged him to start reading the bible and he explained to me what he had learnt from this and we continued meditating on the word on a daily basis for comfort, fulfilment, joy, and peace, which we found over time. He was so intrigued about how Jesus healed the sick that he was able to relate to my situation. Each time we said prayers he was like, 'Jesus was able to heal others and he will heal you too Mum.'

One of the many reasons that made me realise that I needed to take a leap was that I found I was having panic attacks randomly, and this happened about three times, all of which he witnessed. Each time I recovered he would ask me a lot of questions such as if I remembered anything, and how I felt. He told me that he thought I was dying and he was so worried. This was a big wake up call to take ACTION. By taking the advice and instructions from those practitioners that I had opened up to, he was advised on what to do when this happened again. This reassured me and still does to this date.

He is an awesome boy who regularly did most of the household chores including washing the plates and dishes.

He suggested that we should find another solution such as using paper plates and cups so as to reduce our water bills. He would massage my foot with cream, tidy his room and always offer to help whenever I was struggling. Every Thursday he would help with the shopping list and would come up with so many brilliant ideas and optional solutions. He would help me with my shoes as bending was extremely difficult and bring my crutches closer to hand.

I remember when we used to do online shopping. Once, there was a dress I wanted to buy and I asked him what he thought. His response was like, 'Mum, that's a beautiful dress but if I were you I would be thinking of how much money we have in the account. When I grow up and go to work, I will buy it for you but we are practically poor at the moment.' I was so touched by how he reasoned and responded with care and consideration. He was able to forgo most of the things he wanted because he knew we were suffering financially as well which I applauded him for together with being responsible too.

My son, amidst all situations, had encouraged me to meditate, and he created a mental bucket which we filled with our worries, pain, and fear that we used to throw away each time. He constantly researched on how I could get better and gave me ideas for exercises. There were some times when he could not sleep because he needed to know that I was okay and safe; he was a proper gentle, caring, and honest Golden Boy. This was when I was like, things have got really to change and my precious son shouldn't be going through this while I was watching. I had to be brave and say enough is enough.

My son craved for the mum he had before the accident but it was tough. With a lot of effort, I was able to make up games, play Scrabble, draw, and bake cakes which he enjoyed. We even started writing a book which we called 'MLP Dimensions.' We were able to create this environment despite all of the challenges we were facing. This worked well and conjured up many wonderful ideas creating content which we wanted to use to help young minds cope when a parent is facing challenges such as mine. His gorgeous smile would light up the room as he came up with so many ideas that we would work on at some point.

We used to travel to Uganda each year during the summer holidays but we were unable to do so this year 2019. To start off with, my son was not happy when I told him this but he understood and he was able to accept the situation we were in. But this did not stop him from talking about his cousins and grandparents, and the food and fruits he would have been eating or the lifestyle he would have been having whilst in Uganda. I hadn't realised how much he loved going until then, and no wonder he was asking me to teach him my first language which he reminded me that he was learning in order to be able to speak with most of the kids back in Uganda if we had happened to go. Bless him. It appeared to me that it took him a while and he kept thinking about this and really accept it. Nevertheless, he told me not to worry about it but one day, surprisingly before he fell asleep, he told me he had something to say. I was like, 'My ears are all yours, my beloved son.' He said, 'I just want you to know that things will get better and that you should not worry anymore.' He added that it's not that God does not like us but loves us, and he doesn't want me to suffer. He continued to say that most times things happen to us for a reason and that God is testing me to see whether I can persevere and continue to serve and love him. He further went on to say that God wanted him to tell me this! 'Have a good night Mum and may the Holy Spirit and angels protect you and keep you through the night. This came from him, honestly? I couldn't stop crying and he said, 'Mum, are those tears of joy?' I said, 'No, I am not crying.' He got emotional too and hugged me. 'Everything will be alright Mum, we just have to believe and trust in God.'

How I stayed inspired and kept motivated for my revolutionary breakthrough.

I stayed focused and determined and refused to be offended by others. This is because I learned and had the proof that the more I continued to give my heart assignments, the more my heart stopped from looking for assignments elsewhere.

I had to wear a smile and promised to talk to myself as I would to someone I loved for the rest of the month no matter what the challenges.

When my mental and physical health was really bad, I gave myself a break. There was no space for me to allow making myself to feel guilty for things I could not do. I did not feel bad about eating bad foods or about not doing as much as I normally would.

I am human. It's okay to struggle. I had to look after myself and my mind because that's what's most important.

I am so important, that I never notice. I firstly give priority to the others, which is also important but still, I have to understand myself, look after my health, my emotions, and spiritual upliftment. I had to intentionally visualise and remember that I am the brightest star in my own galaxy.

I meditated saying that to be beautiful means to be myself and that I did not have to be accepted by others but instead, I had to accept myself before anyone else.

God shut me in. I had always thought that Noah was safe inside the ark because he built it according to God's specifications. I thought that perhaps it was the strength of the gopher wood and the soundness of the architecture that ensured that the waters of the flood would not come into the ark.

While I was reading my bible, I encountered a verse that shifted this whole paradigm. Genesis 7:16 says, "The animals going in were male and female of every living thing, as God had commanded Noah. THEN GOD SHUT HIM IN." I did not want to miss the fact that even after Noah had built the ark, it was God Himself who shut him in inorder to shut out the waters of the flood!!

It is not the fact that I have locked my house that keeps me safe at night. It is not my good driving that keeps me safe on the road, neither is it my healthy eating habits that keep me healthy. Only God can shut me in and shut out the devil that is seeking to devour me! I prayed for God's protection in everything about me and for my friends and family. For example. 'Father, I pray for my son and other children that in the midst of kidnappers and mistreatment, you protect them. Keep out the flood waters of abuse, rape, murder, car accidents, disease, and death. Shut us into your ark of protection, into your ark of love, into your ark of compassion.' Amen.

I promised myself never to regret being a good person to the wrong people. This is because my behaviour says everything about me and their behaviour says enough about them.

I decided to be friendly with my neighbours, family, and let go of those who hurt me. Be vigilant, have a simple lifestyle, identify my weaknesses, and maintain a conscious mind.

Only I could secure myself and my safety was paramount and no one could protect me.

I hoped to live the life I was proud of, and when I found that I wasn't, I had to gain the strength from anything that made me smile and start all over again.

Success is the sum of small efforts repeated day in and day out. I made myself a note that said, the best time to plant a tree was 20 years ago. The second best is now! Is your time now or in 20 years?

I wanted to be the change I wished to see in the world. It is never too late to be who I might have been so I cried, forgave, learned, and moved on. I let my tears water the seeds of my future happiness.

I had a dream and a big vision to help and inspire others and thought there is nothing more beautiful than someone who goes out of their way to make life beautiful for others. So I did.

I had to do my best then adopt to a 'whatever happens happens' mindset. But I did not try to force things. I just let go and allowed the right blessings to flow. This is because managing whilst living with immobility, chronic pain, stress, and depression are challenging circumstances, but with just a tweak, doing something that excited me uplifted my spirit, hence limiting the stress or beliefs at that point in time. I mean, who wouldn't want this feeling forever? Anything that cheered me up was therapeutic but again, I had to take it one day at a time.

Only I knew what I was dealing with and no one else. I found out that in life there are circumstances we must go through in order to grow or lose in order to gain, and some lessons in life are best learned through overcoming a challenge. I had to live through the worst parts of life so I would never take the best parts for granted.

It's not what I said to everyone else that determines my life, it's what I whispered to myself that had the greatest power.

When I tried to control everything, I enjoyed nothing. Sometimes I just needed to relax, breathe, let go and live in the moment. It made sense to me that every situation in life is temporary. So, when life is good, I made sure I enjoyed and received it fully. And when life was not good, I remembered that it would not last forever and better days were on the way. I did not wish it was easier but wished I was better. I did not wish for less problems but wished for more skills. Did not wish for less challenges but instead wished for more wisdom.

My traumatic experiences taught me lessons that I didn't think I needed to know. I later realised that the situation I was in and the longer I took without action, the more money I was losing and that my dreams and goals we collapsing. I found my purpose through hiding my pain with a smile and started looking for mind alike personalities who were better than me to rock and roll together, who shared my passion for advice, support and encouragement.

I decided to come out and expose myself to my deepest fear of wanting to write this book. After I made the effort of getting to writing and putting my ideas down, fear had no power, and the fear of freedom shrank and vanished. I felt free. I stopped thinking that to be strong is to never feel pain because in reality, the strongest people are the ones who feel it, understand it and accept it. I constantly had a personal reflection every now and then. I had a clear mind and I believed that in order to achieve my goal, I was obliged to define it, want it, believe it, write it down, split it up, review it, schedule it, and make it happen, which pushed me to leave my comfort zone. Dedication, determination, focus, patience, persistence and consistency were paramount. I knew if I could persevere and beat this, it would be difficult for me to give up.

The biggest adventure I took was to live the life of my dreams. In doing so, I did not change my character so people could like me. I had to be myself and ensure that the right people loved the real me. I always remembered that doing what I liked is freedom and liking what I did was happiness. I had the passion, courage, and the fire pressed through and I did not give up until writing this book came true.

I connected with like-minded mind setters. Throughout all conversations I was able to see with loving eyes because life is beautiful. I spoke with a tender voice because life is peaceful. I helped where I could with gentle hands because life is full and because I cared with a compassionate heart. Life turned out to be good beyond all measures. Every time I helped and supported someone else who was going through a challenging situation, the favour was returned to me either directly or indirectly. I could engage in challenges and win memberships for the entire year. Getting vision oriented books from best-selling authors and acquiring the knowhow would equip me to support others and understand human behaviour in all angles of life, even helping those at the very top to have inspiring journeys. This made me strong.

I wanted things to get into perspective so I stopped being afraid of what could go wrong and started being excited about what could go right. I chose to believe in myself because once I became fearless, life became limitless. I chose to be me, do me, and for me.

I knew that when I got the idea of writing this book an opportunity knocked on my door. I had always been willing to take chances simply because I never knew how perfect something could turn out to be. I don't know about you but I used to be an award winning procrastinator. I re-assessed my lifestyle, took action and would never want to go back to where I was. Mind you, I thought I had it all and that I never needed anything more. I was 110% wrong! I was just proud and arrogant. I am saying this because if I had not turned my obstacles into opportunities and my challenges into possibilities, I wouldn't have thought that small opportunities are often the beginning of great achievements.

So, the only way for me was to get what I really wanted and to let go of what I didn't want which would have kept me from making excuses. I never gave up or lost hope. I was able to look back on my life. I realised that every time I thought I was being rejected from something good, I was actually being redirected to something better. Whoever had an input in doing so, this made me feel forever grateful. I knew what I wanted and I visualised seeing it happen. Even though I did not know every step I needed to take, I did not get afraid to get started. I dosed up on inspiration and positivity every day and believed that I would reach my goal. When I had doubts and worries I surrendered them and trusted that everything would work out in the right way at the right time.

I always had it in mind that success wasn't about how much money I made but instead the difference I made in people's lives. When people doubted how far I could go, I decided to go so far that I couldn't hear them anymore and took pride in doing so.

I identified that I would not fail but rather found out 10,000 ways that wouldn't work. I forgot about making mistakes and just did it. I wanted to be this kind of person that made other people step up their game.

I just made it clear to those asking me personally and those who wished to know that I am an open minded individual who was managing to cope and get through life as anyone else. What was UNIQUE about me is my reflective passion and analytical approach of my actions, behaviour, dreams, choices, and goals. My best successes came not on the heels of challenges, pain, trauma, disappointments and failures but through taking action and accepting this...I was A FREE WOMAN with zero regrets. I surrounded myself with various people who were inspired, motivated, open-minded, passionate, and grateful. Believing in nothing is impossible and I was determined to accomplish this while supporting others to do so as well.

I followed my passion and not the pay check because I wanted to be successful. This approach proved to me that entrepreneurs have a mindset that sees the possibilities rather than the problems created by change which is what I continuously followed for this visual and tangible amazing result. I had to think big, visualise, dream, make a plan, take small steps towards my WHY, invest in my personal development, network with those authors I admired and ask questions, and did not listen to people who told me it couldn't be done. I did this because life is extremely precious but short to think SMALL.

The golden opportunity I was seeking was within me but not in my environment. It was not in luck or chance, or the help of others, it was with me alone. So, I did my best until I knew better, then when I knew better, I did better.

I listened to my intuition and trusted myself to create a life that I really wanted to live by stopping to tell myself I didn't know what to do. Yes, I did know.

I starved my distractions and fed my focus. If I did not find a way to make money while I slept then trust me, I would have to work until I die. But I knew I was not here just to make money alone, but to leave a legacy too.

I believed I could and that I was halfway there. This was a proven fact for me to testify that no matter where I came from and what my personal challenges were, my dreams were valid. Period.

I decided that no matter what was happening in my life, I would choose to be happy. This is not because everything was perfect, but because I deserved it. I remembered that I was the main character of my life's story. So I had to focus on giving my audience not only something to look forward to, but something to be inspired by.

I stopped worrying about what I had to lose and started focussing on what I had to gain. I kept calm and carried on despite my ongoing health issues, finances and being jobless. I never wanted to engrave all my challenges upon my heart any longer, simply because I knew if I wanted to let go of them, I wanted to forget them, hence I could not hold on to the hatred of what I was undergoing at the time. This implies that my happiness was not determined by what was happening around me, but rather what was inside of me. I never wanted to depend on others to gain happiness, but instead to come from within. I also took into account that being happy to me was not about everything being perfect but that I needed to look beyond my imperfections.

It came to a time when I realised I was on my own. I cried, felt guilty, regretted, hated, became silent, struggled to forgive, and I covered up but boy, did this help? What I did was to suck it up. I stopped whining, stopped complaining and stopped expecting. This was because in the end, disappointments are inevitable.

Helping and supporting the girl children in need as an ambassador, although not being their mother, I cared for them each day. When I managed to visit them in 2018, I cuddled, sang and read to them and also watched them as they played. I saw each new accomplishment and helped them to grow and learn. I understood their language and I listened with concern. They came to me for comfort, and I kissed away their tears. They proudly showed their work to me and I gave the loudest cheers. No, I am not their mother, but my role is just as strong.

I never wanted to dream about success but rather worked it. I smiled and indicated to everyone that today, I am a lot stronger than I was yesterday. Each time I woke up alive I took deep breaths, relaxed my shoulders and thought about all the things that made me smile. I thought of my favourite colour, taste and smell. I did not need those to live but I had them. I cherished the joys. I remembered that the struggle I was in was developing the strength I needed for TOMORROW.

I understood my worth, valued my life and appreciated my blessings and what I had. I kept my goals where I could see them. I never stopped to think about what I needed to do to love what I did. I learned to take action simply because sharks too have to keep moving to live and I needed to keep moving forward in order for my dreams to live.

I did not need to do anything today, but I did need to do something every day. So I realised that in reality, winners are made not born and I understood that successful people get where they are by following a strategic plan. They learn what it takes to go ahead. Therefore, I understood that to build a house it takes a plan, a blueprint, but I sometimes forget that to build a successful life, it also takes a blueprint. I fondly thought about this to reflect, review, analyse, understand and came to a solution. Therefore, as I grew more certain of my purpose and my talents, I came to rely less on the attitudes and abilities of those around me and more on my own passion and ability. I also focussed on what I believed; that my eyes were placed in front because they are more important to look ahead than to look back.

My best defence was to listen but I never listened when being criticized. To some extent, I displayed some measure of defensiveness, the impulse to reject any and all criticisms by denying validity or undermining the messenger. Unfortunately, defensiveness did not serve me. It encouraged me to ignore potentially useful feedback, which inhibited my abilities to improve. It was good to know that I was capable and showed it. I learned that we shouldn't fight criticism merely because we can.

CHAPTER NINE

Stepping Into My Divine Purpose

Well, this is a very broad topic. I know and I believe that it takes courage to be able to open up about it freely so you can learn to set yourself free. I mean, there's loads of pain, hidden traumas, health concerns, and emotional challenges such as anxiety, stress, depression, and physical challenges, all of which I experienced major symptoms of.

What I have realised is that most times we forget to prioritise ourselves and give too much power and control to the external world who have no idea of what we are really going through and experiencing and as a result, we get really agitated, burn out, experience internal bleeding which wears out us out, and we get fed up as we feel like an absolute failure with no hope.

I mean…I remember when I had my personal injury three years ago. I experienced various traumas and some of them were caused by listening to what some people were saying about me, not being able to open up to tell the truth, and the fear of being judged. This of course caused a lot of pain and suffering. I couldn't weight bear, I was so exhausted and ended up using my elbows to walk at some point. This led me to the extent that I tried to end my own life. Life was too hard and I couldn't find even a little light at the end of the tunnel. I just couldn't think straight.

The ringtones were reminding me that I wasn't good enough. I was judged and I felt that I was being defined by my personal circumstances. I overheard one person in particular talking negatively about me and that made me cry and feel worthless. I kept thinking, why me? How could they do this to me. I was on strong medication that wasn't helping but instead making me feel worse. I was dizzy, having nightmares, gaining weight and I couldn't do much for myself. I kept blaming the people who couldn't understand the situation I was going through, like the medical experts. At one point I considered having my entire leg amputated as the last option as after all, I couldn't bear weight. I had hardly anyone to listen to me and I didn't have a job to go back to.

This caused a lot of anxiety and I could not sleep. I was struggling financially but what was striking me the most was my son who had been a young carer at the age of six. He saw me crying through the pain and struggles. Each time I had a panic attack I remember I would try to have a conversation with him and reassure him that everything would be alright. He would respond by giving me a hug and tell me to thank God that I was still there with him. I would ask, "What do you mean, son?" He would say, ''Mum, when you wouldn't wake up, I thought you were dead." Oh my goodness!!! Again, this would remind me of the person who caused the accident and I would enter into the 'bitter 'mode which never took me anywhere but instead broke me down even more.

I struggled helping my son to do his homework. I was hearing voices of what some people had said about me which wasn't true. For example, one person in particular asked me not to attend their wedding if I was still on crutches because they didn't want their wedding pictures ruined. Someone else said to me that if I went to seek help, no one would believe me because I was psychotic as I had tried to end my life. I had to learn a way of letting go and to forgive them in order to step into my purpose.

There is no way I could have been writing about this had it been that I was still holding on to my past. Seriously, after freeing myself and forgiving everyone else through the process I now share with the people I support, I felt so light and new opportunities started coming my way.

I was amazed that I was taking on so much luggage that wasn't meant to be mine and chaining myself to it. How could I have heard all those ringtones of what other people were saying about me and believed it? Do you at times, if not most times, feel this too? It takes time to accept it I know. It takes courage to acknowledge the damage and the extent to which we have been affected by our personal circumstances which in itself is different from everyone else but if you would love to get better, you must follow the process of someone who has walked the path and seen the results.

Looking back and from the testimonials from the amazing people I have supported, what we struggle with and have had said about us isn't true and for me, I didn't want to be entangled in the same old situation longer than I wanted to be. For this same reason, I made a decision and woke up one day wanting to change my life. All I ever wanted was to be and achieve more, inspire, and empower other people struggling with health concerns. When I attended university and undertook a degree in business management and HR, I was striving for a better future. Upon finishing university I secured a dream job role that was a perfect fit but unfortunately, it ended abruptly because of my health condition.

I also trained as a complementary therapist and this job required me to be physically active, but due to my health struggles, I could not practise. You can tell that despite the fact that I was trying my hardest, my health condition was reminding me of what had caused it each time. I tried even harder by wanting to do more and find something that I could manage around my health then all over a sudden, I saw a course. This was in counselling and listening skills which came in handy after I had been through twenty-four sessions including CBT and EDMR treatments and they hadn't worked well for me. At the back of my mind I knew I wanted to find out the reason why and this came up; here comes the power manifesting into your life.

Even though I undertook the course, I'm not saying it was easy because we all know life is not as easy as we think. A few times during my class I was woken up by the tutor as I had fallen asleep due to the medication that I was on and the pain I was experiencing and each time I was asked to go back home. Well I just couldn't and begged not to because I had found out my WHY. This is so important in our lives despite what we are going through.

This is something the people I support find useful as it is an incredible tool. I found that role-playing between client, observer and counsellor so useful and it made me realise the person I wanted to be. It made me know the person that I was and my capabilities. I was able to be congruent with myself. I was accepted and I was able to be empathetic. This helped me to gain an inner healing. It helped me to identify how to organise myself and to know more about myself and who I really was, and I also identified my weaknesses which I gradually worked on. I felt that I could begin smiling truthfully.

I wanted to have my power and to be in control of my life and own it so that I could be the best mum in the whole world and make my son proud and appreciate him for everything he had done for me and for each individual who had been there and supported me. Never take this lightly.

Can you remember when I mentioned about having my WHY as a strong tool? Well, this is what I meant. Forgiving and letting go to set yourself free so you can step into your divine purpose can take a lot of structured steps and this is what I teach my clients. You'll get to the point where you get to choose to be more and stop blaming others who annoyed, and wronged you or caused you harm and accept the support from those who know more than you do. I opened up and I chose to be myself. I said no matter how long it would take me and that whatever did not kill me would only make me stronger. You might be there thinking that this is too hard. But when you adopt this kind of attitude you will be glad you did. It's one of the systematic tools to enable you to venture into new opportunities.

I remember saying that I couldn't forgive anyone but I never knew that by saying this I was only holding myself back from my destiny. So now that you are reading this, all I'm asking of you is to please put yourself first. Let go of whatever made you cry. Let go of that someone who upset you. Let go of that someone who made you feel bad about yourself. Stop those negative thoughts that weaken you,and makes you feel so angry and bitter. All you have to do is to free yourself and Let Go. If it means crying out loud like a little child then please do so because I did this a number of times myself to release my anger and frustrations. Look up to God Almighty because for me, he was the healer. He granted me all the things I was craving for by allowing me to forgive and ask for forgiveness too through his grace, which opened up new opportunities for me. I found joy, peace, and happiness through his God's grace. You too can experience this if you can breathe in confidence and breathe out all the fear and self-doubt.

I wanted to rise up and be able to open up, speak up, and say the truth without feeling judged. I knew I had to make sure that my voice was heard to be the person I am today. So, if you're on the fence and you feel like it's too hard and you feel suffocated by what you are going through and you need a breakthrough in order to progress, you need to let go so that you can step into your purpose. This can be done in so many ways but if you do not share your story or confront what you are struggling with of which you are the expert, you cannot change your life. You deserve more and I would appreciate it if you could find the way to be the best version of yourself. Trust me, it feels heavenly.

When I am having a 1-2-1 and I am speaking to my clients about this, a number of times they open up to me and say, "Josephine, thank you, and where have you been all along?" In most cases you may not even know that you have had so much pain or think that you needed it or know the extent to which you didn't know yourself until when you get exposed to this. Let me share with you what empowers me when I make a difference in someone else's life.

I remember a lady who was eighty-six years of age when she contacted me. Her family thought she was suffering from dementia. They had diagnosed her with this but that wasn't the case. She did not feel right because of how she was being branded by her own family, to the extent that they were thinking of moving her into a sheltered home and when I heard this, I was able to create a safe space where she openly told me what was wrong and worrying her that no one else seemed to understand. She was sad and angry and she even hated her family. Had it not been that I had experienced my own resonating situation, I would not have been able to support her.

I was able to get her to open up to exactly what she was feeling, why she wasn't attending her medical appointments, and the medication side effects. I gave her plenty of time to express herself and as our meeting carried on, I noticed her calmness and relief and all over a sudden she said, "Josephine, is it okay if I cry?" Of course I granted her this. This was because I had rectified what was wrong with her and made some suggestions and recommendations on how to move forward.

Before the consultation ended she said, "I'm crying simply because you are a black girl and you could potentially be my granddaughter and no one else has ever been able to listen to me. No one could understand me but you have. I must admit at first, I didn't want to tell you anything because I thought you would judge me like other people so I'm so glad I found you." She continued. "I'm so glad you've helped me, I'm so glad you could understand me, thank you so much. What can I give you? How much do you want? You have just saved my life. I mean I'm eight-six but you have been able to understand me and help me to be hopeful. I feel a thousand times better, like I was eighteen again."

I swear, by recalling it now, I can still hear joyous laughter and smiles coming from within. I knew I was hearing someone else's pain and helped her to release that tension and access her intuition with ease. When you do something you love passionately, help someone overcome what they are struggling with, you will help yourself as well by setting yourself because if they smile, you find a purpose. And as a result, this keeps me going and I never ever give up because testimonials are the best things ever. If you ever find yourself stuck and find it extremely hard to let go and free yourself, just do something good for someone else; it yields great outcomes. Always remember this.

I was nominated to be a Girl Child in Need Ambassador in Uganda and by supporting those kids and listening to them, I was given a purpose, and I forgot what I was going through myself simply because I wanted to do more for them even though I didn't have enough myself. Financially, I was able to contribute and campaign so those kids could eat and have the basic scholastic materials for school.

From this point my passion for sharing my story to change my life was born. I'm also now on a mission to impact millions of women who have experienced a traumatising illness to have a safe space where they can freely open up, be heard and get supported without being defined by their situation, and to boost their confidence. I happily share my 8 steps proven journey that I took to let go in order to step into my divine purpose without feeling embarrassed of my story, be scared or hold any grudges against anyone else which resulted into helping to inspire you with it. You too can be a miracle to someone else by sharing you're 'letting go' story, and if you are struggling with this, I'm sure you can reach out to me for more help and support.

CHAPTER TEN

How I Got the Courage to Embrace My Own 8 Pillar Model

Let me think. I am guessing that when you chose to get hold of my book you would want to know my how and why I came up with it. I promise you will get the answer by the end of this chapter. Maybe you are in the middle of the road with so much information that you have absorbed without it taking you anywhere along the way, or it's possible that by reading my story you would think of that one person to recommend my book to. It is also possible that you will start brainstorming your ideas too. Whichever the case may be, trust me, I know how it really feels. I remember wanting to find that one person who would understand and resonate with me without any judgement and to help me overcome what I wanted to achieve. Someone who would want to listen to me and be open about and present with me each time I wanted to speak and share something. I remember having a lot of ideas and writing in any notebook to hand. I had a notebook in the kitchen, in my chest of drawers, on my bed, and in the living room, with a pen alongside each book. Ideas were flowing from the lessons I had learned along the way and thinking of how I would love to help someone else and get my voice out there and be heard. I hated what I was going through and how it affected me to the point that I vowed to go on a mission to help millions of people like you to feel human and embrace what you are struggling with so you can find your personalised help.

It is such a horrible experience to undergo personal struggles alone. Mental pain, physical pain, emotional stress, depression and anxiety. I experienced all these in one go. Yes, I feel you can imagine this. I know that even your closest family and friends may fail to understand the extremes to which you are struggling with. It can be challenging to sit every single person down and explain from start to finish. I know this because I tried my hardest to hide away every struggle to the point that I couldn't do it any longer and I was damaged. I can say that what I was going through I could not even put into words.

In most cases, the people we try to confide in, if there isn't anything in it for them, will judge you, won't see what you are going through as strong enough or serious enough and you will be criticised. I could also hear the words from those I thought would understand and who thought that I was making it all up, and may have defined me as a weak person. At the end of the day, I knew I was human and I was the expert in what I was dealing with but even when I knew this, I personally wanted to impress them which indicated that I had given my power away to them and it showed in another way that I had lost control over my life.

Well for me, this hurt the most and I knew I had to find a way out of my situation. I remembered that they were not in my situation and only found out this after I had embarked on my transitioning journey to recovery. Seriously, if you can understand this better and earlier before the situation and symptoms get worse, the better you can manage the situation and so I decided to step into the gap to create this awareness before it's too late and you lose your loved one's life. Ideally, everyone should be cautious and understand that once someone they know gets ill they go through life challenging situations or struggle with mental health. Their way of thinking and their perspective of how they perceive and understand anything being told to them is different and keeps fluctuating each time.

I remember being there and being present but getting upset and blaming other people simply because someone did not understand me or treated me differently. It is very easy to get yourself into that situation and for me, when I did, I stopped talking about my struggles and allowed people to talk for me and all I could do was listen and not respond, but deep down, I felt deeply bruised and bleeding. You don't have to live such a life. You were not created for this reason and if you are hurting and feeling uncomfortable, whatever the case may be, you have got to confront it immediately, even if it means reaching out to someone you know and if they don't listen, keep searching for that person in order to find the right person who will listen and be there for you. You are so valuable and more precious than you think, and I promise you that when you do find that right person to support you and believe in you and empowers you, despite anything that you are going through, you will feel a major shift within you that will energise you to find your own purpose and the vision and goals that will help you to find new opportunities within your own capability.

You'll recall from earlier in the book about the loss of my job and my financial struggles. I feel that I must tell you about some of the people I encountered at the Job Centre. Those people and their individual circumstances helped me to be the person that I am today and be able to write this book in order to help others

I never really wanted to go to the Job Centre as I felt that the process of making a benefit claim was beyond me at the time but I was told that if I didn't go, my benefit claim would be stopped and I would need to re-apply. I knew there was no way I could go through the same process again and so I literally dragged myself there.

It was such a miserable day. When I got there I sat in the waiting area while I waited to be called in. There were a couple of people before me. I looked around and I noticed that I seemed to be the only grumpy one around. Everyone else was either on their phone or chatting to someone next to them. I found it strange that everyone looked like they enjoyed being there. While I was waiting, a woman stood up and went to sign on. Upon her return she was really happy that she hadn't even done what they had asked her to do the previous two weeks and that she was virtually getting free money. I knew about benefits and my understanding was that it was for people who were in dire need and they needed that income supplement to get back on their feet while they were searching for employment and not for those who were just sitting around doing nothing.

I also overheard someone who was planning what to do with their benefits. It sounded like they were on the phone talking to their dealer about 'scoring a hit'. It quickly clicked in my mind that maybe they were talking about cocaine or some other drug. It was quite obvious that they had already smoked something that day because of the smell of cannabis on them.

Another lady came in and she was having a conversation with someone else. It turned out that she had five kids with another one on the way. I was shocked that she had never worked in all of her life and I heard that each time she was told to find work, she would quickly fall pregnant and say that her pregnancy wasn't treating her well and so was unable to work.

I felt sad and sorry as I looked around and that's when I felt that maybe I could do something to help these people. I looked at myself and thought about them and how I could come up with a workshop to educate them on certain things they could benefit from. It came to my attention how I needed to enlighten them through working with the Job Centre on resolving such a challenge. Although I felt uncomfortable listening to the various conversations, ideas of how I could help started to flow.

I left the place knowing that my life didn't have to be same way and thought of a mission as I couldn't see myself keep sinking like they were. I felt that I was the only person deep down that did not enjoy signing on for the money even though I was entitled to it. I felt that I had something more to give. I was determined to extract myself from this rut, make a future for me and my son and perhaps help others along the way.

I believed that there must be something that could show people how to be in the comfort of their own home and still earn an income. From this point I started thinking outside the box to find how I could be resourceful to my local community. For me, although the money would help a lot, the process of all the form filling and question answering was so exhausting just to receive the benefits I was entitled to. Please don't get me wrong. If you are struggling financially, this is the route you should take and it will really help you.

I had it in my mind that if I could get myself a modified car that I really deserved I'd be able to look after my son and care for the less privileged such as children in need and those women who are going through financial and health challenges, and also those various charity organisations who had helped me get back on my feet. I wanted to demonstrate to people that they could get out of their situation with a clear vision.

I had this plan that worked so well where I would share my number with those I connected with, and every now and then, I would send a message discretely asking them questions that would eventually get them to talk openly to me. I could visualise my plan coming together and I felt really proud as they loved what I was sharing with them and they asked for more information. I used the same approach even when I attended my hospital appointments. I also remember a couple of people who saw me featured in the Ipswich Star newspaper and reached out for some support. Best feeling ever. I found it was something I was called to do as it gave me so much happiness, joy, and contentment. I was giving something I am really passionate about to those who needed it.

Although I was health wise still struggling and many people were asking me what on earth was I on about, it helped me. No one knew or could understand the extent to which this was relieving for me unless they had spoken to me in person. I recall some people saying that I was wasting my time and that they didn't think things would get better any time soon, if they ever would. I was told that everything I was doing would not be believed by anybody because I was psychotic. Some people wanted me to agree with them and believe that what I was embarking on was something that was too hard for me. I actually didn't take this seriously because I knew I had a lot of transferable skills that I had acquired from university and from my work with other reputable organisations. My work was embraced and I was loved so I knew that what was being said about me was not true.

Therefore, when I embarked on helping anyone I found, I did not have any clarity as to how exactly I could help them and didn't have a clear message. I carried on anyway and I would speak to people and ask a few questions that would lead to us talking every time I sat next to someone else that I thought I could help. It gave me great satisfaction when the first person rang me and they recommended someone who they thought I could help. Well, I did and they got amazing results. They had been struggling to find the right person to speak to about their challenges for the past two years but had never found anyone like me who was so open and understanding without any judgment. I felt like my dreams had come true after receiving such feedback that I was not expecting. The thing is, we all most times tend to underestimate ourselves or only carry the negatives.

You should train your mind to block any such negative thoughts and flashbacks so as to make you become unstoppable. We should never underestimate anyone in life. I'm saying this because sometimes we go through various challenges in terms of finance and self-doubts that would just kill us to the core bone if we allow them to.

I was in such a situation and what I did was to look on Facebook. As someone who is into all forms of personal development and the content that is shared on social media such as Facebook, every now and then I would post about various pain points which would result in positive responses. I also commented on other people's content. With experience, I figured out how to join and comment on other Facebook groups and pages. I connected with some amazing people who introduced me to opportunities and challenges that I signed up for.

I participated in so many challenges that gave me a lot of value and in the end, I became an expert. I began winning each time which helped to boost my confidence. I take pride in saying that those challenges changed my life.

There was one in particular called 'Confidence to Get Visible' by Anna Parker-Naples that I undertook with all my heart. I ensured that I completed all the tasks on time while also engaging with everyone else in the group. I was one of the people who contributed massively and at the end of the five days I won the five day challenge simply by taking on board what Anna had emphasised us to do and as a result, I won a full years' membership.

The power of manifestation and taking action of what is being required of us can be extremely rewarding. And I certainly now show people how to get the best of any Facebook challenge without spending a penny. You just have to connect with the right person within the right group to get you started. Therefore, from taking on challenges and getting great results, I now have my own SYSTEM APPROACH that I use to take my soul mate clients on a journey that boosts their self-esteem enabling them to get back on their feet so they get to enjoy their desired lives stronger than ever before supporting them using my own approved system.

My Client 8 Pillar Approach.

1. **Connection**

   This is a very important part. From our initial conversation we both get to feel that we are fit to be working with each other to enable me support you better to achieve your desired results. For me to achieve my breakthrough I had the right people who cheered me on even when they knew I'd had a pretty rough day because they believed in me and I am passionate to do the same for you.

2. **Why**

   Having a strong reason behind what you would love to achieve is something I do not take lightly and in fact, it is the reason why you are reading this book. Without this, you can always fall off the bandwagon and fail to come back on and I would not want this for you.

3. **Story**

   Yes. I had a personal story that had resulted from a personal injury that I had. It affected me so much. This did not affect me alone but also my son, family and friends. Don't be scared or embarrassed about yours because there's someone out there resonating with you and would do anything to help.

4. **Acceptance**
   I knew what I had been through and the impact this had in my life. I also was aware that I couldn't turn the clock back and the only option that was left was to accept and embrace all of it in order to move on.

5. **Perspective**
   This was a revolutionary norm for me but I wanted to be a changed person in order to help other people out there who are in denial and needing that help, my help, hence, everything else I had heard was negative. What had happened to me as a result of the injury laid a strong foundation to become a voice and get heard.

6. **Purpose**
   From going through this self-reflection and knowing the difference I could make to those who will be needing my help, I prioritised them which gave me the courage to carry on. You should never have to feel alone or have the thoughts of ending your own life while there are people like me who have walked the path and can help you overcome your difficult moment.

7. **Resilience**
   My vision and goal felt so strong that I never ever wanted to get back into my major PTSD, depression

and anxiety mode again. I found a very good management approach that anyone could implement without having to leave their home. Once I got this right and it resonated with me in a way that wasn't straining, I knew this was it and that I could take on anything and handle it without having any relapses and if I did, it was so much easier for me to resolve it quickly and got back on track.

8. **Confidence**

   When I implemented the above and knew I was in control, I felt alive and lively. I was able to share my message on social media platforms, connect with more people, people who were struggling with any of the topics I shared who could comfortably reach out and be ready to be supported. The feedback was invaluable and a combination of my entire signature process. It boosted my confidence and I now feel unstoppable to help others overcome and identify their own passions.

CONCLUSION

If you can visualise me for a minute, seriously, I never thought this would happen to me. Deep down when I was asked to be featured, the agreement was about talking about how the charity organisation, with the help of their amazing team, helped and supported me to get back on my feet. I was visited at my home and the conversation went so well that I had to highlight to some extent my soul vision to help others who are struggling and being affected with health limitations.

I know I keep going on about Family First – a charity organisation that was able to literally take me out of what was holding me back. You see, I was at the verge of losing my life and I hated being in that situation, I felt so down and low as at the time it felt like no one was willing to listen to me. My patience to explain anything that I would benefit from was to the maximum limit. I was helped to silence my own voice by really listening and understand how they were planning to help me. Right from the consultation with the team, I was asked how I preferred to be helped? This took a little over an hour as there was lots of pain, panic, tears, pauses and agitation but we got there in the end. I was reassured and over time trust was built, suggestions were much easier to follow. I accepted and allowed to be helped because every time we had a discussion or meeting, I never felt pushed and always was asked about my major concerns which for me eased the severe tension and anger from how I was treated differently previously. Am I right in believing that we all want to feel this way when in need of rescuing?

Upon reading about me and hearing my story, a number of people reached out to share how proud they were of me for how far I had come, and all I kept hearing was "JOSEPHINE; – You are such an inspirational lady to many and you are going to impact millions" which in fact was my dream. After experiencing what I call hell on earth, with all the struggles and problems I encountered, I would never want you, or someone you know to go through it alone and untold. This is where my drive comes from, so I can relieve the pain and understanding to be a voice for others, about what they are going through. After being featured, and having lots of feelings and emotions of people reading about me, I seemed to lose control of my nerves and a bit of shock had set in. At some point I was asking myself, what did I just do? Could I not have kept quiet? Is this something I really wanted? But I knew all was done for a good intention and I had a chance to emphasise my appreciation.

It felt so good when I had about more than two contacts that I did not know and, more from those who knew me was overwhelming! I did not know my story would impact anyone else other than appreciating what a Christian charity organisation – Family First helped to save my life and identify my purpose!

This is a note I wrote to myself that I feel I should share with you in recognition of this achievement. After being featured in the Ipswich Star on the 12/02/2020, which was all because I briefly disclosed how a charitable organisation Family First under their outstanding Coordinator- Michelle Jones had helped me. They supported me for nearly a year to get my life somehow back on track to identify my purpose, even though they could not help with my health side of things, they made sure that how I felt and reacted to certain situations aligned with their goal (Helping Families in Need) This gave me a platform from the comfort of my own home to express myself in a way that defined me, speak the truth about me and what I was going through without feeling judged or under pressure. I mean at some extent I felt like I was overloading them with so much, which was making the situation worse for me, but I was reminded that it was the same reason why they chose to support me, valued and respected what I was undergoing because they really did understand.

I was overly struggling and so what really got me was that they embraced the 2 of my heartfelt core values 1. Acceptance and 2. Empathy with ease, this has now enabled me to embrace my mission to help inspire, empower and encourage others having various difficulties, who are willing and open to reset and change their lives around in a best way possible. I want to be that person they can relate to as someone who has walked the path and still on the journey but mastered how to get through it to still leave live your passion.

This I have learnt is possible by knowing and being aware of the Do's and Don'ts in such situations, life can be a better place to live in despite what you might be going through. Some people who acknowledged me, have reached out and poured out their hearts about their complex challenges and have not been able to come out to talk about them publicly, they are in constant pain and not sure how to express themselves. They feel shy and the carry the fear of being judged as well as not knowing who to confide in, they feel so insecure and unhappy and so I feel blessed when they praise how courageous and strong I am, having spoken to many in this situation the common factor that they have mentioned is how they felt with me and could totally relate whilst feeling inspired by me and asked how I have been able to open up and accept help as this is also a major area where so many still struggle and just wanted to know how I have managed with all the challenges.

Well, with all the information and concerns that have been raised to me, and having been through much personally that they have shared with me, I know there are so many other people feeling the same hence, rather than thinking how I could help them all, I believe sharing this would help many other people to acknowledge that they are not alone even when they feel like it. Especially when you have been known to be strong and this independent person but now having to rely on someone else for help or even accept care and cannot do the things you used to and enjoy. It is difficult seeing other people flourishing and you are in so much pain and agony to accept that you are struggling and need help, it can be really difficult to handle something that has hit you down which creates a lot to be dealing with on your own. I am passionate about inspiring others and help them transform to the best versions of themselves especially where there are visible, or invisible complex health challenges such as disabilities, to enable them to minimise their levels of emotional stress, depression and anxiety.

I am sharing with you 6 top habits that helped me get through what I was dealing with and even up to this moment I refer back to them every now and then, because I know the incredible benefits I have received from practicing them all. When you hold yourself accountable, you will gradually begin to evaluate yourself, put things into consideration which will help you unlock your potential as well as opening up numerous possibilities and opportunities for you too.

Affirmations.

When you practise and train your mind to think positive, you will start to embrace the power of affirmations. The more you keep prophesying to yourself the best things in life, the more chances of attracting them to happen to you. I promise you this made me feel so much better and it was easy to do. Imagine speaking this out loud to yourself:

- Know today is going to be greater than yesterday.
- I can do anything I want to, and I am going to achieve it

I want you to put yourself in a situation of a time when you planned to move out of your parents' house for the first time, you made sure that you did make it happen without fear and had to start from somewhere. It is the same logic you too can use straight away without spending money towards someone to help you figure it out especially when you are living on a strict budget, be kind to yourself and know that there are so many other people who are relying on you or looking up to you. You can also add to your affirmations that you may not be where you want to be but you are not where you used to be. Wake up each morning and say, I am ready for today and I can get through it perfectly OK. If you are reading this, I am extremely proud of you and I want you to know that you are a step forward because so many other people have failed to try taking action into acquiring this knowledge. You are a WINNER and, a massive congratulation to you.

Pacing

It can be overwhelming as a busy multitasking person, maybe you are a parent trying to juggle family, kids, help with homework, shopping, working and having to do this and that without having to stop for a minute while in constant pain, dealing with some form of disability and discomfort. This can be really exhausting, upsetting and makes you feel like wanting to give up on everything. I am a victim of having to deal with all of this and pretended to be a super woman until when I couldn't anymore after my personal Injury. Even though I was in so much pain, the medication I was on was extremely strong and could make me so drowsy if at all I was not sleeping. At times, I could force myself to do everything in one go but the consequences were severe impacting for the next 3- 4 days of the week in bed, tired, burnt out all because I was not being true to myself and circumstance. This was not helping me in any way until when I had an appointment under pain management that took me through pacing which meant, I had to take breaks even with the slightest thing I attempted to do. You need to know you are human and if not careful, it can go horribly wrong, cause frustration, major stress, depression, and anxiety. I am here to take you through this process if you feel you would need clarity on which technique to use to regain your energy without pressure to flawlessly go through it. The moment you master this, the more you will appreciate what you have not in an awfully long time.

Set SMART Goals that applies to you

I take it that you have now decided you are desperately eager to feel happier straight away. You might have heard or be already aware of the setting SMART goals but with this, I am making it really seem simple for you because it's what worked for me and most of the people I have recommended have found it useful with amazing feedback. Please make sure you don't overthink this, just personalise it into your life, no one else is in your shoes, no one knows exactly what you are going through, whether you sleep well or not at all, what you can do and can't or really struggle with on your own. I do not know much about you, but I am confident that you will find this helpful, and we could get to cross paths too. I found that I could not explain all I was going through to anyone and understand, I remember crawling on the floor on my knees and elbows as I did not want to seek for help because I thought I could do it on my own. Pride never took me anywhere but instead caused more stress and frustration as I could not do much and did not want to accept it, I was too hard on me and overstretching to do what I couldn't manage. Give yourself little tasks and appreciate yourself by doing them. I remember not even wanting to come out of bed, did not eat or even dress up. After a lot of mindset work and going through Nuero-Linguistic Programming (NLP) and exercising mindfulness, I knew I never wanted to be in the same situation tomorrow, I wanted to be better and got determined to go whatever it took me that my vision and goals overweight what I was undergoing.

I made sure I was Specific on what it is I wanted to do, Measurable to my capability, Achievable to me, Realistic and Time scale to accomplish it. As long as I knew what I get out of the task I gave myself an allowance due to my health challenges kicking in, if my plan got out of hand, I trained my mind not to be negative about it and continued with it the next day. I understood that I was not in any kind of competition with anyone and it was my race. If you go by this approach, you will be motivated and achieving what you set yourself will make you happier regardless of how long it may take you.

Everything Happens for a Reason

I know what you could be thinking, but trust me, it is true. If you had told me this before my accident in 2017 and after my suffered injuries, there's no way I would have wanted to speak to you ever again because I would have taken it to the extreme. Seriously, I vividly remember a parent that told me face to face after I had some visible improvements that there was a time they saw me and run away as they did not want to even look at me. They thought I had lost it; I was not happy with this and I totally did understand which angle they were standing as they knew me before. On reflecting, I envisioned this myself and it was one of the things that were eating me up. This alone got me thinking and wanting to take a leap of faith no matter the circumstance to work on myself. Had it not been for most of the things that have happened to me, the experiences and the knowledge this equipped me with and the resilience, there's no way I would be here sharing this with you and what the experience has taught me.

Personal development and hanging around or making relationships with those I admire and being able to follow them, accepting or asking help and take their advice on board otherwise I would still be in the muddle puddle or even be dead because life had become worthless. I found a reason to educate myself and motivate myself, became creative to help teach you how it is done through inspiring, empowering you with how to transform your life. It does not take time but rather courage and I am confident that you too can do it because I overcame it. And hence, on a mission to always here for you with a shoulder to cry on should you feel like resonating with me or my story.

Take Care of Yourself

- I am passionate about this practice and so many people take it lightly, but it is paramount that you take it seriously. As I was in constant pain and taking lots of medication, it was very difficult for me to understand the importance of knowing myself really well. We often think that we know what we are doing and know who we are but in reality, the day you identify the difference the more eye opening you will be, your perspective of how you see things and perceive them will be at a greater level, your understanding and analysing a situation will be different too. I swear by this and I know I could have died from this, I was never putting myself as a priority, always considered what other people said about me, wanted to impress yet I was hiding from me. Please be KIND to you not only today or tomorrow but always.
- The more people complimented about how beautiful smile my smile was and lovely teeth, the more my heart internally bled because they did not know what I was going through. I was putting on a show for everyone to think I had it all perfectly in place. This was not a right approach so please if you are doing it, STOP it right now. Choose to be happy and work towards it. It will not happen overnight but a working progress and always makes it bet-

ter when surrounded by mind alike people such as myself who has walked the paths and aware of the Do's and Don'ts.

- As part of my self-care and not so many people talk about it, if you feel like crying for 10-15 minutes even and an hour please do so, it is one of the best therapies I have used and swear by its results to date, find something you used to love before life became in the way such as; listening to music, looking at old pictures, reading old text, going for a walk, doing own makeup, cooking as this may be a new routine to start with as time goes by, you will be cooking on gas. My results were immediate each time and these pushed me through the day to keep positive and enabled me to work on my dream journey. Once your feelings and emotions are in the right place, you would be able to help others even when you are dealing with complex health challenges that are physical.

Stop Blaming Yourself

- You know I was top on the list to self-blaming which led me to start self-harming as well. I regretted why my life had to turn so bitter, why I was constantly in so much pain, why I suffered an accident and mind you I again within a period of nearly 3 years I had a few accident occurrences, I had too many questions with no one to answer me, my mental, psychological and emotional well-being were completely off. I could sleep without eating because I thought no one was helping me and that everything was my fault. Not most of the people who knew me understood or even bothered to listen to me but of course I know, everyone has their priorities and choices and I will never blame anyone. It is your responsibility not to take it on other people if they have not helped you because they are not in your situation but again you shouldn't blame yourself but try to understand how scary, and intimidating it can be for them too especially if they see you going down the lane.

- One of the key tools I embrace with the people I help and support is communication. Always use your voice to speak up no matter what it is. Your voice is so powerful and needs to be listened to. You need to be heard in order to be helped unfortunately. If you continue self-blaming, then this cannot be beneficial to getting you happier straight away. Don't fight battles silently because you are stronger than you realise. Yes, you may feel hurt, have been broken, with a disability, in pain or feel defeated but always remember that every hero has an origin story. I don't know if you are a Christian or not but my prayer for you is that your untold story needs to be heard as opposed to self-blaming to inspire others to speak their truth in order to heal. That you will see purpose through your pain and strength beyond your struggle.

- Know that your pain is accompanied by a promise that something new will be born. Do not let your current situation suffocate your dreams. You will heal your heart when you walk in the dream that God laid on your soul. Note that there is no greater agony than bearing an untold story inside YOU.

The 2020 Lockdown

Well, like any other person or family, employer, the self-employed especially those in travel or employee, who experienced what we can openly call, the extreme of the lockdown, truth be told, we were all heavily affected in one way or the other, even though the situation came like a joke. However, I believe the situation hit so badly the elderly, people with physical disability and those with mental illnesses. Before it sunk into everyone else's brain, I gathered that many people could not understand clearly what was happening, there was a lot of confusion, high levels of stress, anxiety, depression and sadness as a result and I found myself in the same situation. From one person to another who I spoke with, it felt so strong that I needed to do something by offering an open free service that created awareness of how I helped which meant that if someone got value from our virtual talk and they were happy and excited, it would give me joy that I did not prioritise me first or focussed at what I was struggling with. I can confidently confirm that indeed, we heal or ease our pain by putting a smile on other people's faces. I came to this because prior to going into the lockdown, I was not well and in fact I was craving to go out at least independently. It was so, simply because just before Christmas, I had a massive fall. It came about as I was trying to walk using my crutches. I had always been careful when walking as I am not very stable on my feet but upon moving out of my house I noticed I smelt some cleaning detergent and noticed that the floor was wet, yet there was no sign to mention that cleaning was in progress. As I carefully, walked further to find the cleaners, it was too late as I slipped and fell heavily and I bumped my head and injury my left hip, and right hand. This all happened so quickly. I was really pissed off and immediately asked why me again!

I remember being on the floor and crying like a little child. This is because I was relying so much on my affected leg, that was me now on the floor and I just couldn't get up when I tried, and now this was the point when I screamed for help. Fortunately, the cleaners came and tried to pick me up. I was in much pain and agony and the cleaners could not pick me up when they came to my rescue and tried again, and again but there was no way of getting me up still. It was a struggle, so the cleaner swiftly called for more help but still they failed and at this point, I was already exhausted. In that moment, a taxi driver who was waiting for me to go, and pick my son up couldn't wait any longer so, he left and at this moment there was no luck, and an ambulance had to be called which the waiting time was 4 hours on the floor, at this point, it was getting late to pick my son up. My neighbours started coming out, but I remember getting so tired and feeling extremely embarrassed at the same time but thankfully, my neighbours tried as much as they possibly could to make me feel comfortable whilst on the floor in the hall way. It was so disturbing that I could be passed by each time, as I was in the way for two good hours before the ambulance arrived to take me to hospital. I was praying and hoping that nothing was broken and that I will be alright. During this time, my neighbours kept swapping by coming and keeping me company bless them. Don't we all deserve to have super amazing neighbours like mine? Having come through it, I felt so blessed.

So, until when the ambulance came, my neighbours kept checking on me. And of course, at that time, my son was still at school feeling puzzled and getting frustrated that I was getting late. The school had to ring social services and get him somewhere to go. And of course, this is not something I really wanted as I had experience with them previously. So anyway, they found him somewhere to go after ringing the school and letting them know what had happened, and that I needed to go to hospital as a result. Amidst all of this, I was in tears when speaking to the teacher, I just could not hold myself together, but I was reassured that my son will be in good hands as I was helpless. Whilst in the hospital, they took some scans, and they said everything was fine with increased pain and bruises. However at that time, I did not know that I had bumped my head, because I was numb everywhere, I was on high dosage of pain killers due to my right leg, and Heap. When I heard this, I was in desperate need to get back home and be there for my son. Come to think about it, how many times, do you ignore exactly how you feel for someone else? Well, for me, my son comes first in all instances. Are you guilty of this too? On this occasion, I really didn't want my son to be taken elsewhere but he slept over in another home but again, when you are not well, as you know, your options get very restrictive especially if you lose your consciousness that said he came back the following day. This was not that, he did not enjoy being in another home, but kids really do worry when they get to think of what is happened to their parents. It feels out of control and worrying to them too even though most times they will not openly say it.

Just in case you were not aware, this is the number one stress and challenging behaviour trigger to children as well. You must take extra precautions to hear them out. So, from during the 2019 Christmas period, I wasn't able to even use the bathroom, and using my crutches became increasingly difficult for me and but I carried on until a week before lockdown, things were extremely difficult, and hard to ask for help. I felt like I was asking for so much. At the same time, I needed the help as Dani Wallace wrote in her book, 'CLOSED MOUTHS DON'T FED' I had to express how I was struggling. I chose to open up for more help. It was quite a challenge, before I eventually got help which was stressful, but I got there in the end. In the process at some point, I felt like asking for help was bad even when you are entitled to it. From this point, I knew that some people choose to give up or never ask for help and as a last resort people end their lives. But WHY? From a personal experience, when you need help, and you are alone, there is so much forms and calls and answers to provide which can easily drive you mad. This is why I am here to be your point of contact in case of any query with ease on how, and where to find personal help so you can cut away longer paths that could result into not being successful. I still remember it like yesterday, how I fought when got told that they were worried, that I could not look after my son, and that he needed to be elsewhere he could be looked after as it was phrased that I couldn't look after myself. The challenge here was that not because I could not, but simply because a physical health limitation but not that I was abusing him in any way.

I never hid myself from the fact that life was hard and that I was really struggling with my health. This can be a traumatising situation to experience and in fact, if you have no close friends, family, or friends around you to help you could easily loose the plot. I remember staying in bed, and I needed a lot of encouragement, and support to keep carrying on as well as, pretending to compose myself together even though I could see myself going down. We most times see ourselves through this, but we keep strong of which without inner healing we get affected. Like for me, I recall being told that I was scheduled to be taken into hospital, and this I did not agree with. All I needed was somebody to help. So anyway, they had to go through a long process by ringing my surgery, my son's school, the pain management team, the occupational therapist, and the physio. Oh my goodness me this was massively terrifying, but before I started to say anything for someone to hear me out, my son had a family practitioner, who spoke on my behalf about me and my son, and what was going on, she kindly explained to the team how she supported us, they were able to listen and explained that they only wanted to make sure that my son was okay, and alright.

Even though I was supported more from this point on, had it not been that I was consistent and expressing myself about my symptoms, pain and how my disability was affecting me to support my son, and live an independent life, given my record that I suffered from major stress, depression, anxiety and that I had suicidal thoughts that resulted into me overdosing myself at some point, which I felt that a number of times this was used against me, it would have ended up so badly and my son would not have been with me by now. I have learned so many lessons, and reflected thoroughly during this process, and now I can always support you so that, you don't have to suffer as I did with clear instructions, and recommendations for you that I can help you with in a logic ease way without having to offend anyone else.

How Passion, And Courage Gave Me, A Second Chance, To Live.

I felt that by coming out in the open, to share what has worked for me made such a huge difference in someone else's life. You never know, who is reading or watching you, know how badly they have been waiting to hear a confirmation from someone else, they can resonate with. So, I believe that sharing is caring, and it also become apparent in my life that, when you share your story, you can change your life too. I am a massive advocate and fun for this phrase. I say this because, I shared a post on a social media platform about what I had sewed and what had inspired me, and I got lots of engagement which was mind-blowing and exciting at the same time. At this point, I was contacted by Altovise Pelzer- the Voice manager who indicated that what I had written was inspirational, and that she would love to feature me in her blog of 'YOUR VOICE Matters', and indeed I needed my voice to matter. We had been friends on social media, and we were both following and supporting each other through sharing each other's content and commenting too. And this post was like a BOMB to get us working together more closely. This is the beginning where you too, need to be visible and acknowledged. I chose to be part of this because I am on a mission to empower, inspire and enlighten millions of women especially, those who are ambitious but suffering, and struggling to manage or cope with any kind of health condition either, mental or physical, on how being courageous and passionate, about achieving what your heart desires are, despite what you might be going through, to enormously reward you beyond measure, mentally, financially and socially with a positive mindset and understand that you too can thrive again.

Prior to embarking on this journey, I was dreading about not having a job anymore, what kind of job would I really fit into, I felt so limited and uninspired yet, I know I am quite a bubbly person but couldn't feel it anymore. As you may already tell from reading my previous chapters, my life was tremendously changed after my injury in 2017, from not being able to do most of my daily activities that I used to do and enjoyed, to my life being restricted, and I had no job to get back to as a result. As someone who used to be independent and workaholic more like, this was straining me, at all levels. Amidst the whole transitioning of my life, I remember being severely depressed, stressed, frustrated, agitated and fed up, I used to have panic attacks and I was diagnosed with a lot health conditions such as a neurological dysfunctional syndrome which over time was realised it was one of the medication symptoms I was on, Complex

Pain Regional Syndrome (CRPS) in addition to having the mobility issues and other health complications. This was extremely challenging and really struggled, to accept my situation which brought more damage, and affected the perspective on how I was viewing things.

And what made it worse, each time I attended a doctor's appointment, I would be told that I was under pain management, from them I was sign posted to physiotherapy who would not even do anything due to the extreme of pain I had, and could scream in so much agony if they did any exercise, I had another group of experts who were suggesting the increase of my medication each time from tramadol- which nearly killed me, to gabapentin, to pregabalin, and amitriptyline. Surely, if you have ever been on any of these medications you would know what I mean on the side effects; loss of appetite, gained a lot of weight, anxiety, mood swings too.

The counselling I received only worked during the session, and the moment I was out of the room, it felt like the world was falling apart. I could only hear voices telling me, what was the point for being alive, I cried my eyes out, I did not feel worthy, my heart was scarred and felt like it was cut open each time and it was bleeding, no one had an idea of what was happening to me, there seemed to be so many injustices and unfairness in various aspects of my life and health wise too. I was blaming everyone I saw or ignored me. So, I knew I had to find a purpose despite my severe health challenges, and I was so determined to make it happen. I knew my son needed me the most and it crossed my mind that everything happens for a reason. I now know this, and embrace it gracefully, and I use my proven approach, to inspire, and empower those close to me, behind this saying. I take pride in this because people have reaped good results.

In fact, I knew I wanted more, deserved more and was better than I thought, as various people were complimenting how strong, brave and inspirational I was, and in fact my confidence was boosted more after my lecturer and students nominated me as the most inspirational student of the year. Because I came out and chose to be vulnerable, I knew with my condition and the fact that I was in and out of hospital, sitting still in the 9-5 job and how demanding work is, my analysis on this was not viable.

I wanted to feel normal, and took an action that did not seem to make sense at that time but, by allowing myself to align with the vibration of myself, to feel a sense of freedom, and inner peace that was unlike anything else. It felt so good, I felt happy, and fulfilled. I can promise you that you should not compromise it. I really want you to know, and understand that when you get to resonate with this, it wouldn't matter about how quick you get there, as long as you do get there, and know that, you are not in any type of competition with anyone else. Just wake up, make a decision, and go for your dreams by just doing it.

I recall being in so much pain, frustrated, burn out, did not feel listened to, and was fed up of taking much medication that wasn't doing much to me apart from being in more agony. I hated the feeling of this…from nowhere I went online and researched on a few things I was interested in, and could concentrate on but at the same time make me feel better in the process, I found a course that intrigued me that I enquired more of, was happy to invest in, and went and pursued it which equipped me with the fashion, design and sewing skills, that I never imagined I could ever have or pick interest in my entire life. I mean out of the entire class, I was the only person who never knew how to thread a needle and it was a struggle, but I never shied away and because of my hunger for this, and perseverance, I was able to gain more than all that I wanted to achieve. I found passion in sewing, and I related to it as an inner healing therapy which enabled me to concentrate, and forget about everything else that was happening, and by the time my pain went worse I had that kind of relief somehow, as sitting for long as well caused me discomfort. I persevered and was determined to be certified so I could do something in my own time when I could.

However, upon the course's completion, I put everything aside and forgot about it for some time, out of the blue a friend of mine called to check on me, and as we were talking she went on and asked how I was getting on with my sewing, I was like not really, and that I had left doing it as I didn't have the sewing machine. I really wanted but I had lost the momentum too. I told her the description of what I wanted and oh my days - I had not realised she was taking notes!!! One day she asked if I was at home as she was around my area, I said yes and guess what? She had bought the sewing machine for me and declined me to pay her. A note to yourself, when you are talking, sometimes those we talk to may not seem as they are listening, but some really do. My friend reminded me that she got inspired by me, she was touched by my genuineness, and that she always looked forward to coming to classes because of me too. It was a happy day for me as someone else who was on the course, the same day called me, and highlighted that she still recalled my words and the daily simple step by step manageable approaches and tips I shared with her that she hadn't found it elsewhere at no cost. Hearing this, meant the world to me and I patted myself on the back, built our friendship and trust which resulted into a now a happy paying client of mine. I just want to mention that when you are you, share your story and people understand your message well, they will be attracted to you like bees on honey, and would want to work with you even without having to ask them or chase them. If I hadn't taken the path of sewing, how would this have happened? Never doubt your little inner voice and if you are unsure, always reach out to someone who inspires you.

The fact that I never looked down on anyone, never judged anyone, and that I accepted both of them and did not behave in a way that was not relatable, meant the world to me and empowered me to keep changing my life around in a positive way. Always treat others as you would love to be treated. I was super excited that people believed in me and found value and purpose to move on with their lives with lots of other compliments, and I helped them get through those limiting blocks which we all get every now and then. When I received this feedback, this gave me a big push, a big reason to keep going and that I was believed in even when I did not feel like it. I was able to make my first made bag that someone offered to pay me £15. Since then, I have continued to make more, make dresses, alterations whilst doing something I love, and enjoy, helped heal while relaxing and generating me a passive income too, and hopefully, I'll be introducing my membership on mentoring in sewing with amazing new projects in the near future. The total joy, satisfaction, and fulfilment of this as a result is beyond describable and I know, it would not have been possible without my initial action to allowing myself to accept my genuine potential to make it happen. Yes, you too can, in whatever you set your mind out to do. You just have to trust your gut instinct and go for it. Always remember that one step at a time. Slowly but steadily will get you there.

Let me share with you my 5 actionable tips to help you take action if you are dealing with any challenging situation: feeling stuck, fed up, unsure, feeling lonely, burn out or unmotivated to achieving your personal goals.

1. Sit down, close your eyes, and relax to avoid any destruction.
2. Ensure that while your eyes are closed, you use your finger to touch the middle tip of your nose and let your eyes concentrate on where your finger is. Inhale deeply and exhale up to 20 seconds twice
3. You should be feeling a shift within yourself and feel more relaxed. Now, think of one thing that you would like to achieve, ask yourself, can you do it yourself or do you know someone who can help, and support you achieve it.
4. If you are in doubt, or feeling stuck, be brave and strong to reach out or connect with this person to support you so you can make it happen.
5. Ask questions if you are unsure, and remember that the universe will welcome you the way you are, for who you are too, and grant you what you would love to achieve. After this, I would highly recommend you repeat tip number 2 and wait about a minute before getting up.

I would be more than humbled to connect with you, and excited to hear about how my 5 tips have been of an impact to you. As for me, they have become my second nature.

Here are **My Absolute 10 Tips To Help You Find Genuine Happiness Despite What You Could Be Going Through Instantly.**

https://josephinesandracoaching.co.uk/

ABOUT THE AUTHOR

Josephine S.N Kalagira is a Mother, Author, Speaker, Setback to Comeback Coach, Mentor & Consultant, a Roman Catholic Christian who has had to overcome challenging circumstances to becoming a voice for those who have experienced a setback in life. Josephine has unfortunately had numerous serious challenging episodes of setbacks, having experienced multiple injuries which caused a damaging impact on her life heavily. The result of this injury deprived her from living life as she once knew it. Her mobility was affected, and she became wheelchair bound, which then resulted in her eight-year-old son becoming a carer at an early age. Josephine was diagnosed with a functional neurological disorder and other medical complications, alongside symptoms of severe major PTSD, Depression and Anxiety as well as suicidal tendencies and on a number of occasions tried to end her life as she felt like it was the only way out. Thankfully Josephine has been able to apply various techniques and strategies that has helped her to overcome those difficult moments and now believes, that GOD wanted to take her through this route so, He could nurture and channel her to save others by being a voice to the helpless as she is now aware, and has walked to the journey. Josephine believes strongly that if your Why is strong enough you can overcome anything and that is the passion that propels her to make an impact to the lives of others.

Don't let difficult times, define your destiny

"When life throws you lemons you make lemonade"

— Elbert Hubbard

Printed in Poland
by Amazon Fulfillment
Poland Sp. z o.o., Wrocław

62148163R00113